GOOD AS GOLD?

How We Lost Our Gold Reserves and Destroyed the Dollar

CHRIS WEBER

Manufactured in the United States of America

ISBN: 1456586548
ISBN-13: 9781456586546

Praise for Getting Rich Outside the Dollar

"Must reading for all serious investors. In an interesting, lively style, Weber and Reiss tell what factors drive currencies, economies, and stock markets—and what this all means for Americans... .I would advise investors to pay close attention to what Wever and Reiss have to say—it could prove financially rewarding."

–Albert J. Fredman, coauthor of *Investing in Closed End Funds* and *How Mutual Funds Work*

"Excellent....Opens the minds of American investors to endless opportunities for making money outside the U.S. and outside the U.S. dollar. Citing explicit ways to invest, the book shows how to multiply profits by investing in fast-growing economies and at the same time make extra profots when the currencies of those markets become more valuable against the dollar. To my knowledge, no other book has ever done this before."

–Edgar Gunther, Ph.D., International Financial Adviser

"Weber can write like a dream, and here he lets the readers in on his secrets in highly readable and sparkling prose. For anyone interested in conserving or expanding his capital in today's increasingly complex and tangled world, this book is a must!"

–Murray N. Rothbard, author of *America's Great Depression* and *What Has Government Done to Our Money?*

"Weber and Reiss' book is the best primer available on the way the currency markets work. It's full of good, practical suggestions on how average people can make sure they're not only not hurt by fluctuations in currencies, but can profit from them."

–Doug Casey, author of *Crisis Investing* and *Crisis Investing for the Rest of the '90s*

"I truly enjoyed reading this new book—one of the most thorough and certainly most up-to-date primers on foreign exchange and overseas investing for individuals. The authors correctly point out the long-term forces that will tend to make the dollar less valuable over time. And before laying out specific investment advice, they give one a rare chance to see each of the major world currencies from its historic perspective and to appreciate just how differently each country values its currency."

**–F. Mark Turner, Chief Investment Officer
and Managing Director/Global Bonds
Putnam Investments**

"The authors have done a superb job of making the complex world of currencies and currency trading readily comprehensible to the ordinary investor. The book is full of insights and practical information."

**–Adrian Day, author of *International
Intvesment Opportunities* and editor of
Adrian Day's Investment Analyst newsletter**

"A thorough overview of an important topic."

**–John Rekenthaler,
editor of *Morningstar Mutual Funds***

"There are tips to prosperity on every page... assumes no prior knowledge and talks in every day language. Weber has long advised multimillionaires and bankers. Now let him advise you."

–Andrea Millen Rich, Laissez Faire Books

ACKNOWLEDGMENTS

This book has been decades in the making. This is because of a few people who labored long and hard to find out the truth of exactly what has happened to the gold that was confiscated from Americans in 1933 and then stored in Fort Knox. Some of these people were elected officials; most of them were "only" concerned citizens who over the last three generations tried the best they could to find out the truth.

I have to especially thank Mrs. Betty Racer of Berryville, Virginia, who spent years collecting and scanning all of the documents I've used in this book. They are now deposited at Hillsdale College in Michigan. During all the time I worked with her and her associates, they personified everything that good citizens should be. If ever the truth comes out, it will be because of the groundwork that they laid.

FOREWORD

For most of my life, an interest in gold and sound money was widely seen as a curiosity. Now, a decade into the 21st century, popular fascination with the "barbarous relic" appears more pronounced than since 1934, when FDR seized gold from the private hands of American citizens. The price it commands is at an all-time high. Central banks and foreigners are shifting their confidence away from the dollar and other fiat currencies, and toward precious metals, buying up gold more rapidly than in generations. Prompted by the financial collapse and recession of the last few years, investors, the public, and international experts are for the first time questioning the Federal Reserve and the U.S. dollar as the world's reserve currency. The prospects for dramatic change in monetary affairs seem much better than throughout my entire career. Meanwhile, the threats to the global economy at this most precarious time are as serious as ever.

Many are starting to realize that the stock market crash of 2007 and the painful bursting of the housing bubble did not occur in a vacuum. For most of American history, the U.S. government was held back in its inflationary ambitions by the vital, traditional limits of the gold standard. How we got to this point, where our dollar is backed by nothing but the hollow promises of politicians and the blood and sweat of future taxpayers, is a story still unknown to most Americans. Chris Weber's *Good as Gold*, now in its updated second edition, fills in much of the neglected modern history.

Nowadays, with gold traded freely in the United States, we often forget how rapidly it went from being a privately held commodity to being nationalized during the New Deal. Most are unaware that after World War II, the U.S. government had over two-thirds of the world's gold, only to lose the lion's share abroad—almost half of it in the years from 1961 to 1972—due to the habit of politicians to print ever more money for ever more government spending rather than live within our means as a nation. We forget that the unprecedented era of pure fiat money in which we now find ourselves only began in 1973, when Nixon closed the gold window, reneging on America's promise to the world that our dollar was as good as gold.

Weber also paints a devastating picture of the total lack of transparency involved. In 1953 Fort Knox underwent an "audit" unworthy of the name, as only a fraction of the gold was examined at all, and only a miniscule portion of that was assayed properly. In 1974 and onward, more shell games were played to obscure the true nature of U.S. gold holdings. One Treasury Secretary after another has engaged in doublespeak to distract taxpayers from the truth: That the U.S. government seized Americans' gold and squandered most of it with their inflationary schemes. Politicians and elite opinion-makers shrug off what little we have learned about the poor purity of what remains in our vaults, the scandalous incidents of theft by trusted officials and the mysteries of obfuscatory balance sheets and Treasury documents. It's time for a full independent audit and inventory, and as Weber reminds us, there are numerous time-honored independent firms and newly available technology to make the process non-invasive, inexpensive and reliable.

In this concise book, Weber explains the reality of inflation as a monetary mechanism, shows how much our dollar has depreciated, and exposes such failed experiments as the London Gold Pool of the 1960s and the gradual betrayal of Americans' trust in Washington to safeguard their currency. Common economic myths and fallacies are confronted along the way.

From $35 an ounce, a figure artificially maintained for decades, to today's market price of more than $1400, the trajectory of gold prices tells us that the fiat dollar is disturbingly unstable, and central banks and public treasuries ought never be given a free pass to act with so much power and in secret. All who wish to restore freedom, or simply avoid national bankruptcy, must learn the importance of monetary affairs and the war on sound money and

economic reality that our politicians have been
waging for a lifetime. In this vein, *Good as Gold*
is an important read and a wonderful addition to
your bookshelf.

Rep. Ron Paul (R-TX)
Washington, D C February 1, 2011

PREFACE

The story you are about to read is shocking. It is also tragic and sad. It is the story of how the American people's money was confiscated, and what happened to it afterward, as far as we know. History tells us that in 1933, supposedly to fight the Great Depression, all Americans were commanded to turn in their gold coins and bars. They got the grand sum of $20.67 for each ounce. Almost 80 years later, each one of those $20 gold coins is worth around $1,500. And the $20 and change in paper money they received would today maybe buy a cheap, plactic children's toy. Further, that toy would probably be made in China, which has become not only the world's largest gold producer, but whose government buys up all of the gold mined there, and also buys tons each year on the open market. As it has throughout history, gold flows to nations that are ascending.

In the meantime, what was in 1949 the greatest amount of gold ever assembled in one place--Fort Knox--saw at least 80% of that gold go overseas. This was done in pursuit of a policy that even the most Keynesian of Keynesians thought was wrong, as did the great free-market economists of that time.

Officially, the US still has the most gold of any nation. But we don't know that for sure, and we don't know the quality of whatever gold is left. The most we have is a few clues. For instance, the Washington regional director of the US General Accounting Office revealed in a letter that less than 10% of that gold is of a quality that is of a purity high enough to be called "good delivery".

Just how much gold remains in Fort Knox? I have in this book used the U.S.government's own statements, both public and private. What emerges is a pattern of an institution with something to hide. At least, they have consistently <u>acted</u> as if they had something to hide. In all the years since 1933, there has never been a public audit worthy of the name. Instead, we've been handed evasions, ridicule, and outright lies.

It is long past time for the lights to be shined into the vaults. For wherever the truth shows us, we must be ready to handle it.

I have purposefully not used footnotes to document the numerous government statements in this book. Instead, with the Internet, anyone can find the actual documents themselves. They are all gathered in one place, and all available to be seen online. For instance, to see the letter written by the GAO's Hyman Krieger that basically reveals just how bad the quality of any remaining gold in Fort Knox gold, do the following:

Go to the Hillsdale College Library Special Collection Archive at HYPERLINK "http://www.hillsdalecollege.edu/library/Archives/index.html"www.hillsdalecollege.edu/library/Archives/index.html. Then, scroll down to Special Collections and click on George E Durell Collection. Once there, in the box marked For:_____, type in the name of (in this case) Hyman Krieger. Finally, scroll down until you find the date April 11, 1975. Click one last time, and the letter appears. Do this for the author and date of any other document referred to or quoted in this book.

You may be angry at what you read here. Or the story may sicken you. But the technology now exists to easily find the truth. All that is lacking is both the pressure and the will.

"... [the] growth in foreign dollar holdings [has] placed upon the United States a special responsibility-that of maintaining the dollar as the principal reserve currency of the free world. This required that the dollar be considered by many countries to be as good as gold. It is our responsibility to sustain this confidence."

John F. Kennedy, 1961

TABLE OF CONTENTS

Introduction

THE IMPORTANCE OF GOLD

Before 1971, gold was the legal linchpin of the world monetary system. Although every currency was defined in terms of the dollar, the dollar itself was defined as 1/35th of an ounce of gold. The international system worked because the dollar was convertible into gold—at least by foreigners.

However, Americans couldn't turn their dollars into gold at any price; they were prohibited from owning it. In pursuit of a disastrous policy that tried to assert that the dollar was more important than gold, the U.S. government confiscated the American people's gold in 1934 and embarked on a path that would divest the nation of two-thirds of its gold reserves over the next 37 years.

In 1950, U.S. depositories held more gold than had ever been assembled in one place. Throughout the 1950s and '60s, the U.S. government exchanged one ounce of gold for $35—despite the fact that more dollars were being printed than our gold reserves warranted.

On August 15, 1971, the U.S. defaulted on its promise to pay gold for dollars. It finally admitted that all the U.S. dollars in existence could not be exchanged for gold at $35 an ounce. There were just too many dollars and too little gold. This realization came too late, for by then 400 million ounces of gold—two-thirds of the nation's reserves—were gone.

In just the last few years, however, there has been a renewed interest in gold. Important molders of public opinion, some government officials, and even the President of the World Bank are finally coming to realize what average people the world over never forgot: that gold is the ultimate store of value and the essential element in monetary and economic stability. As former Chairman of the Federal Reserve Alan Greenspan put it, "Gold is the ultimate money."

It now makes sense, therefore, to ask what happened to the huge gold stock the U.S. once had. How was its loss explained? What is the status of the gold that remains? Why has there been no transparency from the very beginning?

In this book, I have let U.S. government officials attempt to answer these questions in their own words. What their responses revealed was shocking to me, and I hope they will shock you, too. When you have finished reading this extraordinary tale of official lies, evasions, and incompetence, you will agree that there must be an investigation to discover what really happened to our national treasure.

Historical Background

It is important to realize how the piece of paper we call the dollar began. Papers marked "dollar" had no value in and of themselves. They existed only as convenient ways to carry a receipt for gold. When the U.S. dollar was established under the Coinage Act of 1792 it was defined as 24.75 grains of pure gold. This amount equals 0.0565 troy ounces and would today be worth almost $80 at current gold prices. The Federal Reserve Notes in our pocket today are not dollars in the pre-1933 sense. In that year they stopped being redeemable in gold by the American people. Today's U.S. dollar is not defined in terms of gold or indeed anything else. It is a promise to pay nothing. This book adheres to the convention of calling these unbacked, irredeemable notes "dollars," but we trust you will know what is meant.

After World War II, the United States dollar became the world's primary or "reserve" money, not gold. All foreign currencies were defined in terms of the dollar. Even gold was priced in dollars. From 1933 to 1971, an ounce of gold was valued at $35. For 40 years, despite a massive inflation of paper dollars created out of thin air by the Federal Reserve System, the U.S. government stubbornly insisted that an ounce of gold was worth $35; no less, and certainly no more.

In the 1960s, smart foreigners saw what was happening. Washington may have said that the dollar was as good as gold, but Europeans, Asians and even Soviets disagreed. History had taught them that gold retains its value long after paper promises are broken.

So, during most of the 1960s, foreigners exercised their rights to receive one ounce of Fort Knox gold for every $35 they presented to the U.S. Treasury. Americans, however, were prohibited from doing so. Huge amounts of gold flowed out of the U.S. Treasury in the 1960s, and more was auctioned off in the 1970s, into the hands of those in foreign countries who appreciated its true value.

At its peak in 1949, Fort Knox held 702 million ounces of gold. By 1971, only 291 million ounces were left. The questions: Why did the government permit this massive loss of the country's gold stock?

"A Barbarous Relic"

Few American voices were raised in protest, because, again, Americans had generally been conditioned to view gold as (to use economist John Maynard Keynes' phrase) a "barbarous relic." Americans had also been conditioned to accept the deficit spending and inflationist policies—called "Keynesianism"—that cost us more than half our nation's gold and seriously harmed our economy in the process.

These policies allowed politicians to print and spend paper money they could not redeem in gold, causing price inflation and federal budget deficits to soar. And when the Department of the Treasury finally admitted, albeit indirectly, that the dollar was not sufficiently backed by gold (or anything else besides the good will of the U.S. government), they simply stopped paying it out. Since then, the price of gold has soared almost 4,000%, from $35 in 1971 to—at this writing—around $1400 an ounce. Ever since, the government has officially valued the gold it has left at a mere $42.22 per ounce. In other words, we have the absurd situtation where $42.22 is the price at which the U.S. Treasury will **not** sell its gold.

Where Did Our Nation's Gold Go?
The Treasury Department's Curious Silence

Despite increasing American interest in gold, most citizens still believe that the nation's gold reserves are immensely large and have been prudently managed. However, the facts tell a different story.

FACT: From 1958 to 1968, 52% of the nation's gold reserves left this country.

FACT: These shipments were made with the knowledge and acquiescence of government officials.

FACT: Since the confiscated gold was sent to Fort Knox in the late 1930s, the government has

never conducted a full physical inventory, at least one that was made public.

FACT: Inquiries into the history of America's gold reserves and the policies behind that history have been consistently stonewalled.

Many citizens have begun asking how so much gold could have been allowed to leave our vaults— and why what remains is of inferior quality. Straight answers to the questions and, most importantly, a true and independent physical inventory would quell any doubt. That the Department of the Treasury has chosen not to respond in this way, can only lead an objective observer to wonder if something may be wrong.

Hundreds of attempts have been made by private citizens to have the Treasury Department clear the air. Over the years, about 500 different government officials, both elected and appointed, have been asked to help resolve this controversy once and for all. In nearly every case, the questions were met with either silence or evasion. Not only have interested private citizens been given a brush-off, but even members of Congress who have attempted to investigate have often met a stone wall.

Of course, the Treasury's tight-lipped response has raised some eyebrows. If the people's gold is all accounted for, why don't those responsible prove it? Why do they continue to meet relatively simple questions with complex, evasive answers?

Americans once believed what their government told them. But too many things have happened in too many areas for this any longer to be so. We have been made skeptical, if not cynical. Having lost more than half our gold reserves, we should not have to rely upon unverified Treasury Department claims about the amount and the quality of what gold is left.

There should be a physical inventory—by independent accountants—of the gold supply, and this should be done immediately.

Part I

Gold stored in U.S. Depositories is in the form of bars such as the one pictured. Markings include a seal to identify the smelter, indicating when and where the bar was cast, a number showing the recorded purity (999.9 fine), and a number used to identify a group of bars from a single pouring. (Reprinted with permission from *The Courier-Journal* and *The Louisville Times*)

Chapter One

THE FIRST STEP

Our story begins on April 5, 1933. On that day, President Franklin Delano Roosevelt, just one month in office, outlawed private ownership of all gold bullion and all gold coins over $100 face value (with the exception of rare coins). Most of the gold in private hands was in the form of gold coins. The new decree was, in effect, a confiscation: Those who didn't comply were subject to as much as ten years in prison and a $10,000 fine. In today's terms, this would perhaps be nearly $700,000 considering that the price of gold then was $20.66 per ounce compared with today's price of about $1400.

Those turning in gold were paid the official price for it: $20.66 per ounce. After they did so, the official price was raised to $35 per ounce in 1935. However, only foreigners could turn their dollars into gold at the higher price. At that time, there was an incentive for them to do so since the $35 price was much higher than the prevailing market price. President Roosevelt apparently picked the new price at random one morning at breakfast. It became a sacred figure, however, and in years to come millions of gold ounces would be spent in an ultimately unsuccessful attempt to maintain it.

The American people lost something important when they lost their right to convert paper money into gold at the U.S. Treasury: They lost their ability to limit the government's power to manipulate the purchasing power of their money. They also lost the power to restrain unchecked government spending.

When people had the ability to redeem their paper dollars for gold, there was a limit to how much paper money the government could print and spend. It is no accident that the government has felt itself free to inflate since then. By any measure, the dollar has lost over 90% of its pre-1933 value.

The Centralization of Gold

The official reason for prohibiting private gold ownership was to give the government a centralized arsenal with which to defend the dollar. The coins were melted down into bars and a new maximum-security facility was built to house the huge hoard. This was the United States Bullion Depository at Fort Knox, near Louisville, Kentucky. This inland location was selected, according to news reports of the time, as a safeguard against possible invasion of the seaboard cities, namely New York City and Philadelphia, where gold had been warehoused. No expense was spared in making this depository impregnable: Roof and walls were layers of steel and cement thick enough to resist aerial attack; electrified, reinforced steel fences and guarded "pill boxes" provided assurance against ground assault. It was speculated that half the world's gold supply would soon be safely warehoused in the new facility.

American citizens were given until April 28, 1935 to surrender their gold. Construction of Fort Knox was completed in 1936; by the end of 1937 the gold had arrived.

Because of the high price offered by the U.S. Treasury and the safe haven status of the United States during World War II, by 1945 Fort Knox's vaults were bulging with the most gold ever assembled in one place. In 1933, the U.S. Treasury held 33.5% of the world's gold. By war's end in 1945, the figure was 59.5%. The peak was reached in 1949, when the U.S. government had 702 million ounces in the vaults: a mammoth 69.9% of the whole world's supply, and far more gold than had ever been assembled by one owner since recorded time began.

By 1979, that hoard had shrunk to less than half its peak. Further, there are questions about both the quality and the amount that remains. In any event, the U.S. government is no longer the major player it once was in the world gold markets. In what seems like a foolish move today, it disposed of gold at unrealistically low prices. And, because it did so, the nation no longer has the power it once did to control its own monetary, fiscal, and economic future.

Chapter Two

THE 1953 "AUDIT"

Hours after Republican Dwight Eisenhower became President in January of 1953, he ordered an audit of the nation's gold reserves. There had been 20 years of government by Democrats, and many Americans wanted to be certain that those responsible for confiscating the people's gold had taken proper care of it.

In many ways, this audit fell short. It certainly was not an independent audit, and it most likely wasn't a complete inventory and assaying. Popular sentiment as well as Eisenhower's response clearly had the best interest of the nation at heart, but in retrospect, the audit raises more questions than it answered.

There were efforts to make this audit seem independent, but they were really only cosmetic. An Advisory Committee comprised, with one exception, of private sector bankers and businessmen was responsible for setting up the rules regarding how the accounting would take place. The Committee Chairman was W. L. Hemingway, Chairman of the Executive Committee of the

Mercantile Trust Company, St. Louis. The other members were William Fulton Kurtz, Chairman of the Board, The Pennsylvania Company, Philadelphia; Sidney B. Congdon, President, National City Bank of Cleveland, Cleveland; James L. Robertson, Member of the Board of Governors, Federal Reserve System, Washington.

All of these men, however, had been appointed to the Committee by Eisenhower's Treasury Secretary George M. Humphrey and his predecessor, Truman's Treasury Secretary John W. Snyder. So, despite Eisenhower's professed intentions to make a clean start, the audit began by allowing former members of the very group (the U.S. Treasury), which, in effect, was being audited to oversee the rules of that audit. In short, they were auditing themselves.

Not surprisingly, the "continuing committee" chosen by the Advisory Committee to conduct the audit was made up of three persons under the government's control. One represented current Secretary Humphrey (Maurice M. Washburn of the Comptroller of the Currency's office), one represented former Secretary Snyder (Eugene G. Shreve of the Bureau of Printing and Engraving) , and one represented the quasi-independent office of Treasurer of the United States (George Reeves of the General Counsel's office).

This group, in turn, chose about 400 government bureaucrats to conduct or oversee the audit.

According to the Treasury's press release of April 12, 1953:

"Approximately 370 employees of the Treasury Department, drafted from the Bureau of the Mint, Office of the Treasurer of the United States and Bureau of the Public Debt, participated in the audit. Thirty employees of the General Accounting Office were assigned by the Comptroller General of the United States to observe and review the work done at each of the various audit sites."

The very next—and last—sentence of that press release is amazing:

"All Treasury employees participating in the audit were assigned to activities other than those on which they are regularly employed."

If the government wanted experts to conduct the audit, why not let the bureaucrats investigate the areas in which they had the most expertise? And if the government wanted *objective* investigations, why not call in truly objective auditors—outside experts from the private sector?

Results of the 7-Day Audit

Eisenhower was sworn in on January 20, 1953; the official audit results were "revealed . . . at the close of business January 27, 1953." For some reason, it took until April 12 for the Treasury Department to issue its official press release, which announced:

"An audit report submitted by a *Special Committee* appointed jointly by Secretary Humphrey and former Secretary Snyder revealed total asset values in the official accounts of the Treasurer of the United States at the close of business *January 27, 1953* amounted to $30,442,415,581.70, consisting of gold bullion $23,035,947,570.94; silver bullion $2,154,542,328.37; bank deposits $4,748,638,098.56; and coin and currency, etc. $503,287,583.82."

The official report of this audit found that what was on record as being there was in fact there:

"Secretary of the Treasury Humphrey announced today [April 12, 1953] that an audit and test count of the gold and silver bullion holdings of the government has shown these holdings to be intact and the Treasury records of them correct."

How Much Gold Was Audited?

As strange as it seems, it is still not clear exactly how much of the nation's gold supply was audited in 1953. Reports vary from a 5% sampling of the stock to a full 100% physical inventory.

To clarify this matter, let us go back to the Treasury's official news release at the time, printed in most of America's Sunday papers on April 12, 1953:

"At the Fort Knox gold depository, where the *records showed* $12,483,415,360.28 in gold bullion to be stored in sealed compartments, *several compartments were opened* in accordance with agreed-on spot-check procedures and the gold bars counted. The count of approximately 86,000 bars, amounting to 34,399,629,685/1000 fine ounces, valued at $1,203,987,038.28, was in exact agreement with the recorded contents of the compartments.

"Approximately 9,000 bars [about 10% of the total], amounting to about 130 tons, were weighed on special balance scales of high sensitivity indicating exact weights to the hundredth part of a troy ounce, and again the results were in exact agreement with the records.

"As a final step in the verification procedures the Fort Knox Special Settlement Committee had *test assays made of 26 gold bars* selected at random from the gold which had been counted. The results of the assays indicated that all gold tested was of a fineness equal to that appearing in the mint records and stamped on the particular bars tested. Gold samples used for the test assays were obtained by drilling from both the top and bottom of representative gold bars.

"In confirmation of the verification of gold bullion asset values held in the Fort Knox depository the Special Settlement Committee reported, in part, as follows:

"On the basis of assays, your Committee can positively report that the gold represented, according to assay, is at the Depository. *We have no reason, whatsoever; to believe other than, should all melts be assayed, the results would be the same.*

'We, the undersigned, found the assets verified to be in full agreement with the assets as indicated by the Joint Seals affixed to the respective compartments on January 26, 1953.

'It is the opinion of this Committee that the same agreement would be found should all of the compartments be verified."

It is clear that this press release asserts that there was not a 100% inventory. They say only that "several" of the sealed compartments were opened and their contents counted in spot-checks. Then, just over 10% of those spot-checked bars were weighed. Finally, less than one third of one percent of those bars were assayed.

We must rely on the *opinion* of the Committee that if all the gold had been tested the results would have confirmed the records.

Consistent with this position are the statements of Treasury Department official Jerry H. Nisenson, Deputy Director for Gold Market Activities at the Office of Foreign Exchange Operations, who took office in the 1970s. In several letters to concerned citizens he stated that only 5% of the gold was audited. For example, in a March 13, 1981 letters to a Mr. L. Hendricks of Lincoln, Nebraska, Nisenson stated: "Although the 1953 audit, to which you referred, was also performed in accordance with accepted auditing standards, it was only a partial audit covering 5% of the U.S. gold stock."

In fact, it seems that at some point in the early 1970s (after the 1974 audit, certainly), Treasury spokesmen themselves said that only 5% was audited back in 1953, perhaps to make the 1974 audit seem more complete. For example, Bill Humbert, the Chief of Internal Audit of the Bureau of the Mint, claimed on June 4, 1975 that the 1974 audit "included more gold bars than the one in 1953."

What the Audit Revealed

Certain facts are clear from the 1953 audit:

Representatives of the audited group were allowed to help make the rules governing the audit.

The government bureaucrats involved were inexperienced in their tasks.

The entire audit lasted only seven days.

Only a fraction of the gold was actually tested.

Based on that fraction, the official committee reported that, in their *opinion,* all the holdings would have matched their records if they'd been tested.

Finally, whatever the accuracy of the 1953 audit, the fact remains that at least 59% of our nation's gold flowed out of Fort Knox in the years following the audit. In fact, if there is a possibility that the audit was *inaccurate,* and the amount of gold held at that time was overstated, then we might find that an even greater percentage left this country.

These facts raise many troubling questions which must be explored.

Chapter Three

TRANSITION TO TROUBLE: 1953-1961

The 1953 audit may or may not have been an accurate one, but it did quiet fears about the gold supply. Such an audit today would not have done so, but in 1953, before Vietnam and Watergate, government pronouncements were believed without question.

Meanwhile, events quietly took place over the next few years, which would result in massive losses to our gold supply.

A government can slap a price on any commodity; that price does not have to correspond with economic reality. However, if it does not, economic law tells us that certain things will happen. If the government sets the price too high, people will rush to sell that item to the government. If, for example, the government decrees that it will buy apples for $1 each when the market price has been 25 cents, obviously apples will pour into the government barns as long as the real market price is lower.

The same is true with gold. Even though the government had fixed the gold price since World War I, there had been a market price for gold. In 1934, when the official government gold price was raised from $20.66 per ounce to $35, the government price became higher than the market price. Gold poured into Fort Knox and continued doing so through the end of the 1940s. However, during all this time the government was systematically depreciating the purchasing power of the dollar through inflation. Inflation of course results in more dollars needed to buy the same item. And yet, the government refused to acknowledge this inflation by raising the official price of gold.

We don't know (and cannot know) at what point the official $35 gold price corresponded exactly to what the market was willing to pay. We know that in 1932 the market price of gold was about $20 and by 2011 had gone above $1400. Past inflation, fear of future inflation, and general lack of confidence in the U.S. dollar had all combined to cause the price to soar.

TABLE A

Excerpt from: U.S. Treasury Department News Release,
December 11, 1981, page 22

U.S. Gold Stock 1944-November 1981   (millions of fine troy ounces)

Gold Stock	Net Sales or Purchases				
Year	Outstanding end of period	Change during period	Foreign Countries	Gold Pool	IMF	Domestic Producers & Consumers
1944	589.5					
1945	573.8	.15.7	-12.9	–	–	-2.8
1946	591.6	+17.8	+20.6	–	–	-2.8
1947	653.4	+61.8	+81.8		-19.6	-0.4
1948	697.1	+43.7	+43.1			+0.6
1949	701.8	+4.7	+5.5			-0.8
1950	652.0	-49.8	-49.3			-0.5
1951	653.5	-1.5	+2.2			-0.7
1952	664.3	+10.8	-11.3			-0.5
1953	631.2	-33.1	-33.3			+0.2
1954	622.7	-8.5	-9.3			+0.8
1955	621.5	-1.1	-1.9			+0.8
1956	630.2	+8.7	+2.3		+5.7	+0.7
1957	653.1	+22.8	+4.9		+17.1	+0.8
1958	588.1	-65.0	-65.5			+0.5
1959	557.3	-30.7	-28.5		-1.3	-0.9
1960	508.7	-48.7	-56.3		+8.6	-1.0
1961	484.2	-24.5	-27.5	-0.3	+4.3	-1.0
1962	458.8	-25.4	-21.3	-2.5		-1.6
1963	445.6	-13.2	-19.2	+8.0		-2.0
1964	442.0	-3.6	-12.3	+11.2		-2.5
1965	394.5	-47.6	-37.8		-6.4	-3.4
1966	378.1	-16.3	-13.9	-3.4	+5.1	-4.1
1967	344.7	-33.4	+2.9	-32.3	+0.6	-4.6
1968	311.2	-33.5	-6.0	-25.9[2]	-0.1	-1.5[2]

1969	338.8	+27.6	+27.3		+0.3	
1970	316.3	-22.5	-18.0		-4.5	
1971	291.6	-24.7	-24.1		-0.6	
1972	276.0	-15.6	-0.1		-15.5	
1973	276.0					
1974	276.0					
1975	274.7	-1.3				-1.3[3]
1976	274.7					
1977	277.6	+2.9			+2.9	
1978	274.9	-2.7			-1.4	-4.1[3]
1979	264.6	-10.3			+1.4	-11.7[3]
1980	264.3	-0.3				-0.3[4]
1981-Nov	264.1	-0.2				-0.2[4]
		-325.4	**-235.3**	**-45.2**	**-0.6**	**-44.3**

We don't know exactly where the two lines crossed and inflation made the dollar actually worth less than 1/35 of one ounce of gold. But we do know that, at some point, $35 gold became an unrealistically low price. At that point, many people realized that, regardless of what the government said, an ounce of gold was actually more valuable than 35 paper dollars.

One way to tell when gold became worth more than $35 an ounce is to look at the amount of gold flowing into and out of the official U.S. coffers. Since the U.S. Treasury stood ready to exchange one ounce of gold for every $35 presented to it, it stands to reason that we would experience a net loss of gold once its market value exceeded $35.

The Tide Turned in 1958

One look at Table A pinpoints 1958 as the turning point. At the end of 1957, the U.S. gold supply was still high, at 653.1 million ounces. But beginning in 1958, gold was rapidly drained from Fort Knox. Over the next three years, to the end of 1960, the U.S. lost almost 150 million ounces (a record 65 million in 1958, 31 million in 1959, and 49 million in 1960).

The same story is told from a different perspective in Table B. This table shows the dollar value of the nation's gold in relation to the foreign holdings of dollars. In 1955, the U.S. held $21.8 billion worth of gold to cover $11.9 billion in dollars held by foreigners. The U.S. could have redeemed all that with no problem. But precisely because the U.S. had much more gold than paper claims on that gold, foreigners did not try to redeem their paper dollars. As the U.S. paper money supply increased, however, it was a different story. Foreigners watched from 1952 to 1957 as the supply of dollars continued to rise. In 1958 they began to claim gold.

The chart shows that 1958 was the last year in which foreigners could have theoretically turned in all the dollars they held and received U.S. gold. By 1959 the U.S. government was no longer able to meet its promise to redeem all foreign-held dollars for gold. As long as gold was "worth $35," there were too many dollars and not enough gold.

TABLE B

U.S. Gold and Foreign Dollar Holdings 1949-1959
(billions of dollars)

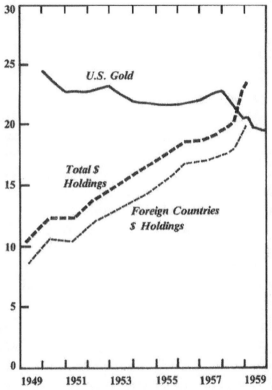

Source: Robert Triffin, Gold and the Dollar Crisis, The Future of Convertibility, (New Haven: Yale University Press, 1960).

Political Embarrassment or International Bankruptcy?

At that point, the U.S. essentially faced two choices: political embarrassment or international bankruptcy. It could stand by its promise to make the dollar as good as gold or it could abandon that promise. If it chose to keep its pledge, it would have to raise the official gold price, by then a quarter of a century old, to account for a quarter century of inflation. Had the price been doubled right then to $70, the gold stock in 1959 would have been worth $40 billion, or almost twice the supply of foreign-held dollars. The problem with that, in the politicians' view, was that this act would be tantamount to a 50% devaluation of the dollar. (That is, instead of a dollar being worth 1/35th of a gold ounce, it would now be worth only 1/70th of an ounce.) This, or any devaluation, would be *a major political embarrassment*, an international admission that the U.S. monetary house had not been in order. And, unless the government reformed, the risk was that at some future point further devaluation would be necessary.

If, on the other hand, the U.S. chose to abandon its pledge to redeem the dollar with gold, not only would this be *an admission of international bankruptcy*, but it would also throw the world monetary system (based, as it was, on dollar/gold interconvertibility) into chaos.

Neither choice was politically palatable, but sooner or later one of those paths had to be followed to achieve monetary stability for the country. At the time, many supposed experts argued that the U.S. could avoid the harsh realities, and since neither option was attractive, the government chose the path of least resistance—it did nothing to reform the monetary system. Instead, the policy of allowing a massive gold drain was continued.

By the end of Eisenhower's term in 1960, the problem was obvious. Gold was flowing out; foreign liabilities ($18.7 billion) clearly exceeded the gold stock ($17.8 billion); and the market price of gold was trading as much as 10% higher than the unrealistically fixed $35 price.

This, then, set the scene for the response of the new President John F. Kennedy, who inherited the problem when he took the oath of office in January 1961.

Chapter Four

Kennedy Inherits the Problem —And Makes It Worse

On February 6, 1961, two weeks after he was inaugurated, President Kennedy sent a message to Congress which addressed the issue of gold outflow. It is a fascinating document in that it crystallizes the consensus of "Establishment" economic thinking at this critical period. Contributing to it were economists John Kenneth Galbraith, James Tobin, and Walter Heller, as well as financiers Douglas Dillon and Robert Roosa. All these men were Kennedy's advisors, either in the Treasury Department or the White House. Dillon was Secretary of Treasury and had served in Eisenhower's cabinet, changing political parties to serve with Kennedy. Roosa was Undersecretary for Monetary Affairs; Galbraith, Heller and Tobin were economic advisors.

This document gave the best summary of the attitude of official Washington at the time, and provided the reasons for what they were about to do, namely: to form the London Gold Pool.

From our vantage point all these decades later, Kennedy's message boils down to two essentials:

First, he blamed the problem on almost everything except the actual culprit—the inflationary and irresponsible creation of paper money. Secondly, he pledged to meet the problem by, essentially, dumping enough gold onto the market to reassure foreigners that the dollar was "as good as gold."

He began his statement by blaming the gold loss on the balance of payments deficit. (In other words, more money was flowing out of the U.S. than was coming into it.) This idea was authored by Galbraith, who later admitted that "I was exaggerating the issue of the balance of payments deficits."

In fact, the deficit was the result of our dollar/gold policies, not the cause. The deficit was caused by dollars flowing out of the country—which, in turn, was caused by an excessive creation of dollars flooding the U.S. and the world markets. The culprit was inflation.

In any event, Kennedy said "The loss of gold is naturally important to us . . . (the) growth in foreign dollar holdings (has) placed upon the United States a special responsibility—that of maintaining the dollar as the principal reserve currency of the free world. *This required that the dollar be considered by many countries to be as good as gold. It is our responsibility to sustain this confidence.*"

"However," he continued, "our fundamental economic position is sound; the dollar will be supported. Our gold supply is one of the factors which lend basic support to our monetary and financial position. Our gold reserve now stands at $17.5 billion. This is more than 1-1/2 times foreign official dollar holdings and more than 90 percent of all foreign dollar holdings. [A few years before it had been over 200% of total foreign holdings; 90% was nothing to brag about.—Author's note] It is some two-fifths of the gold stock of the entire free world." But this figure would soon change, due directly to what Kennedy said next:

"Of this $17.5 billion, gold reserves not committed against either currency or deposits account for nearly $6 billion. The remaining $11.5 billion are held under existing regulations as a reserve against Federal Reserve currency and deposits. *But these, too, can be freed to sustain the value of the dollar; and I have pledged that the full strength of our total gold stocks* and other international reserves *stands behind the value of the dollar for use if needed*."

He later listed six "firm conclusions" and of those conclusions, only number one has importance:

"1. The United States official dollar price of gold *can and will be maintained at $35.00 an ounce.* Exchange controls over trade and investment will not be invoked. Our national security and economic assistance programs will be carried forward. Those *who fear weakness in the dollar will find their fears unfounded. Those who hope for* *speculative reasons for an increase in the price of gold will find their hopes in vain."*

This was, in fact, an open and irresistible invitation to speculators. Kennedy committed the U.S. to a policy of "freeing" (i.e., dumping) as much gold onto the market as necessary to deny reality. The reality was that, due to the printing of new paper money, someday the dollar would have to be devalued and the official gold price increased. *By defending an indefensibly high dollar value— by dumping gold—Kennedy set the scene for the policy that would rob the U.S. of almost half her official gold from 1961 to 1972 (from 509 million ounces to 276 million ounces).*

Avoiding the Problem

It is interesting, if sad, to examine all the measures Kennedy proposed to solve the gold outflow and the payments deficit. There were no less than 18 proposals. Each avoids the real solution, which is: The only way to increase the value of the dollar is to halt the creation of so many dollars.

Many of the proposals listed here in brief actually went into effect, but to no avail:

Improve international monetary institutions. This would result in the creation of the ill-fated London Gold Pool (see Chapter Five).
Borrow money from the International Monetary Fund. That is, go into debt even more to shore up the dollar.

Institute special high interest rates on dollar bonds held by foreign governments. The idea was to make dollars more attractive to own and to stop foreigners from claiming gold.

Prohibit holding of gold abroad by Americans. This had just become law under Eisenhower. Until then, Americans, while prohibited from owning gold domestically, could still use the loophole of legally holding gold abroad.

Kennedy's full comments on this bear reprinting. "The recent Executive Order forbidding the holding of gold abroad by Americans will be maintained. It was fully justified on grounds of equity. It will also help to prevent speculation in the gold market. I am directing the Secretary of the Treasury to keep me advised on steps being taken for effective enforcement. I place everyone on notice that those few American citizens who are tempted to speculate against the dollar will not profit in this manner."

This law was unenforceable. Private Americans acting through Swiss bank accounts, for instance, could and certainly did continue to buy and hold gold, almost certainly some of it from Fort Knox. They were breaking no Swiss law by doing so; they were thereby entitled to protection under Swiss banking secrecy laws.

Kennedy's next 14 proposals were designed to stem the flow of dollars overseas:

Approve and join the Organization for Economic Cooperation and Development (the OECD). Still in existence, it is the "club" for industrialized countries. Its purpose, said Kennedy, is to "provide a solid framework within which we can carry out intensive and frequent international consultations on the financial and monetary policies which must be pursued in order to achieve and maintain better balance in the international payments position."

Promote U.S. exports. Decades later, we still hear this cosmetic proposal trotted out to solve basic U.S. spending and inflation problems.

Stabilize costs and prices. "Our export promotion efforts," said Kennedy, "no matter how well devised or energetically pursued, will not be effective unless American goods are competitively priced. Our domestic policies—of government, of business, and of labor—must be directed to maintaining competitive costs, improving productivity and stabilizing or where possible lowering prices. Measures to achieve these ends which are important for the domestic economy are even more vital for our international competitive position. I have already stated my intention of creating an Advisory Committee on Labor and Management Policy to encourage productivity gains, advance automation and encourage sound wage policies and price stability."

Once again, Kennedy—like Nixon a decade later—addressed the effects of inflation, instead of the *cause*. Inflation *causes* prices and wages to rise. It is futile to try to stabilize or lower these without addressing inflation's fundamental cause: excessive money creation.

Finance and guarantee exports through the Export-Import Bank. This bank was and is a boondoggle whereby taxpayers subsidize favored companies that would otherwise be unable to compete in the world trade market. Through it, countless billions have been wasted with no real benefits to the dollar or economy as a whole.

Increase "foreign travel to the U.S." This is one of the more laughable solutions proposed. The idea is that if we simplified our visa procedures and advertised abroad the benefits of travel to the U.S., this would help solve the basic problem of overinflating the dollar.

Expand agricultural exports.

Assist foreigners in buying U.S. goods. In other words, lend them taxpayer money so that they can buy products of uneconomic U.S. companies. This opens up the same can of worms as the Export-Import Bank proposals.

Reduce tariffs and discriminations against American exports. This is, in fact, a laudable measure, even though it didn't (and wouldn't) address the basic problem. Years later, Washington is still proposing it.

Promote foreign investments in the U.S.

"Abuse of 'tax havens' taxation of American investment abroad." Kennedy stated: "I shall recommend that the Congress enact legislation to prevent the abuse of foreign 'tax havens' by American capital abroad as a means of tax avoidance. In addition, I have asked the Secretary of the Treasury to report by April 1 on whether present tax laws may be stimulating in undue amounts the flow of American capital to the industrial countries abroad through special preferential treatment, and to report further on what remedial action may be required. But we shall not penalize legitimate private investment abroad, which will strengthen our trade and currency in future years." This, in fact, resulted in a measure, the Interest-Equalization treaty, which crippled U.S. investment abroad. All these decades later, higher inflation, deficit spending and taxes (all exacerbated by a lack of gold backing to our currency, and no gold discipline on our government spending) have almost certainly increased the use of tax havens far beyond what it was in 1961.

Contribute foreign assistance to the less developed countries. Assist less developed countries so that they can one day buy from us.

Reduce "customs exemption for returning American travelers." Kennedy explained: "After World War II, as part of our efforts to relieve the dollar shortage which then plagued the world, Congress provided for two additional increases of $300 and $100 in the duty-free allowance for returning travelers, for a total of $500. The primary purpose of this change having vanished, *I am recommending legislation to withdraw this stimulus to American spending abroad and return to the historic basic duty-free allowance of $100.*" This is the most pathetic "solution" of all. Taxing returning American tourists by reducing the duty-free limit from $500 to $100 really avoids the problem.

Centralize review of dollar outlays. To cut back on government spending overseas.

Try to save on military personnel spending abroad, by limiting personal spending by them while overseas.

There you have it, the president of the United States blaming everyone and everything: speculators, U.S. tourists, foreign tourists, tax evaders, wage and price raisers, even drafted U.S. soldiers and their families abroad. Only the real cause escaped blame, or indeed any mention at all. It´s no surprise that all the measures proposed that day failed, when enacted, to make a dent in the problem.

Nevertheless, with this message Kennedy set the stage for the organization of an international government framework whose purpose it would be to transfer millions of ounces of U.S. gold overseas.

Part II

Chapter Five

FALLING INTO THE LONDON GOLD POOL

The free market gold price began to cool off right after Kennedy's message, with his forceful pledge to defend the dollar and preserve the $35 per ounce price with whatever it took. Private demand for gold subsided to where, by mid-1961, the open market price settled back to the official $35 price. (It had been over $41.) Part of this was due to initial confidence in Kennedy's message. But it was also because central banks soon stopped buying gold on the open market.

This limited cooperation among governments quickly expanded and became institutionalized in October of 1961, with the establishment of the London Gold Pool. It was called the "London" pool because London was the site of the physical gold trading. And it was called a "pool" because 8 nations pooled their resources to stabilize the gold price at $35 an ounce. They agreed not just to stop buying gold themselves, but also to be ready to sell gold onto the market when the price threatened to rise.

The U.S. was required to put up half the gold necessary for the pool's operation. The other seven nations (France, Belgium, Italy, Germany, Holland, Switzerland, and the United Kingdom) jointly provided the other half. The gold was physically removed from each country to the Bank of England, wich acted as agent for them all.

In 1962, the market cooled enough to allow banks to buy gold as well. Until 1965, all seemed to go well, by Kennedy's standards at least. Granted, the gold stocks of the nations decreased a bit, but the $35 price was kept stable rather easily. The figures of U.S. official gold loss tell the story: After losing almost 150 million ounces in the three years before 1961, 1961's loss was "only" 24.5 million ounces, 1962's was 25.4 million, 1963's was 13.2 million, and 1964 saw a meager 3.6 million ounces leave the U.S. While this four-year loss of about 67 million ounces didn't please anyone, at least the rate of loss had slowed from the late Eisenhower years. The crisis faded from the position of importance it had assumed. But not for long.

Warning Bells Were Sounded

Even during what appeared to be the system's heyday, a few intuitive people sounded warnings. One of them was monetary expert John Exter. In a May 1962 address, Exter charged that the dumping of gold on the market meant "the very lifeblood of our economy is being drained away."

He was particularly concerned by the type of people who were getting the gold. "Our monetary laws, as presently established, make it easy for our enemies to drain off—directly or indirectly—billions [of dollars worth] of our gold and to use it not only to bulwark their own economies, but mainly to undermine our free way of living and to harm us in every possible way... As things stand now, *speculators, including Americans, who are prohibited by law to acquire or own gold, are purchasing and hoarding substantial quantities of gold in world markets*, such as in London, Zurich, Stockholm and other principal cities. These speculators can well afford to pay a slightly higher price than the equivalent of $35 per ounce of gold, for does not the United States guarantee the $35 gold price to all comers by its policy of buying gold at that price?"

So, America's policy of selling gold at artificially low rates was helping some of the very people the policy had been designed to thwart. Every foreign country, friend or foe in the Cold War, was given an opportunity to drain the nation's monetary heritage away. And speculators were being handed a sure thing. Those sophisticated enough to look beyond the U.S. government's official policy knew that the $35 level was a denial of economic reality, which could not be maintained. They were more than ready to cash in on America's mistake.

Did Americans Buy Fort Knox Gold?

Who bought America's gold? We have noted that it was illegal for Americans to buy gold abroad—but did some do so anyway? (Plus, remember that before around 1960 it was completely legal for Americans to own gold overseas as we saw in the last chapter. There is not one case on record where the American government compelled any American to bring back the gold that they had purchased and stored overseas.)

The assertion that some Americans were buying U.S. gold overseas by 1962—by which time it had become illegal—is an interesting one. Though they would be breaking U.S. law by doing so, any American who really wanted to could—and did—buy gold overseas. There is no record of any U.S. citizen ever being prosecuted for doing so, but it is certain that some Americans did break this unenforced, indeed unenforceable, law by buying Gold Pool gold in the 1960s.

In the early 1960's, I myself heard about an elderly friend of my family who was heiress to a large fortune. She was convinced both that the U.S. was making a mistake in selling off its gold and that Communists and international bankers *(some of them American)* were getting our gold. So she decided to buy up as much gold as she could herself to prevent at least some of it from falling into the "wrong hands." This was easy for her, as she spent part of the year in Switzerland anyway.

Not only was she never caught, she lived to see her holdings soar in value twenty-fold when gold reached $800 per ounce in 1980, and used her gains to support the causes she believed in.

What about her claim that American financiers were also buying U.S. gold surreptitiously? Fort Knox gold shipped to the London Gold Pool was expressly designed to be sold to foreign brokers, individuals, or governments. We know that, using foreign brokers as intermediaries, Americans *were* secretly buying Gold Pool gold in the 1960s. And, further, American financiers and government officials *could* have been among them, secretly feathering their own nest and breaking the very law they had themselves made. (It has since come to light that many in the CIA who routinely dealt with countries where only gold was accepted kept their own supplies all over the world.)

Even a Keynesian Warns of Trouble

Even though John Maynard Keynes had called gold a "barbarous relic" and advocated the inflationist and deficit spending policies that were now causing the gold outflow, there is evidence that during the last month of his life in 1945 he reconsidered.

Actually, Keynes himself was not as anti-gold as many believed even though his followers usually are. In his 1934 *Treatise on Money, Employment and Interest* he called gold "fairly successful over longish periods in maintaining a reasonable stability of purchasing." He also said it "... keeps slovenly currency systems up to the mark. It limits the discretion and feters the independent action of the Government or Central Bank of any country which has bound itself to the international gold standard."

By the early 1960's, Sir Roy Harrod, John Maynard Keynes' longtime student, official biographer, and "keeper of the flame," had sensed trouble ahead if the dollar price of gold was not doubled to $70. In a letter to Undersecretary of Treasury Robert Roosa on January 13, 1962 (just months after the Pool began), he poured scorn on the very idea of central banks cooperating to support an outdated $35 gold price. His last paragraph to Roosa read: "Despite your persuasive account of what has been done in the field of international monetary co-operation, which in my lingo, I describe as 'scraping the barrel,' I remain of the opinion that things will not go well, unless the dollar price of gold is doubled, with the sterling price ditto and the D-mark price up by 80% etc."

In other words, Harrod wanted Washington to follow the realistic path of devaluing both the dollar and the pound by 50% against gold, and, reflecting Germany's better inflation record, devaluing the mark by somewhat less.

There is no record of a reply to this advice, but obviously it went unheeded.

Why Can't Americans Own Gold?

As the outflow of bargain gold continued, some Americans began to ask: "Why are only foreigners allowed to buy our gold? Why can't individual Americans get some of it?" A newspaper editor in Denver named Frank Lily wrote and open letter to the President in early May of 1962 which said, in part: "I find that there is a rapidly increasing number of American people who are asking why they, as citizens of the world's leading free nation are denied the ages-old free man's right to own gold in view of the FACT that this right is being exercised by a large majority of the free-world nations, notably France and West Germany. They frankly ask: 'Why shouldn't our government trust us to own gold as well as sleeping pills, shotguns, brick-bats and whiskey?' you, of course, can recall when it was a crime to own whiskey anywhere in our country but both legal and highly commendable to own any amount of gold. Now that our people are denied under penalty of law to possess gold, can it be truly said that ours is a free nation? Oh for a modicum of uncommon common sense consistency!

"Where is the gain for our people, Mr. President, in providing a sound dollar only for foreigners and thereby running the risk of 'burying' our economy in an avalanche of DEBT?"

Congressman Richard Hanna of Ohio passed this open letter on to Treasury Secretary Douglas Dillon. On June 5 he received a response from Dillon's assistant, Joseph Barr:

"Mr. Lily asks *why the U.S. Government should not trust individuals to own gold.* Mr. Lily will, know, from previous correspondence with the Treasury Department, that we believe that gold's leading role is to serve as a method of settlement in the international payments system. Indeed, as Secretary Dillon stressed to the Ninth Annual Monetary Conference of the American Bankers Association in Rome on May 18, 1962, '*the Free World's monetary system,* as it has evolved since World War I, *rests fundamentally on the full acceptability of the dollar as a supplement to gold* in financing world trade.' [i.e., That people should accept the dollar as they would gold because the dollar is, they said, as *good as gold*.] No practicable alternative is in sight. This means that the dollar holdings of central banks must continue, in the future as in the past, to be readily convertible into gold upon demand at the fixed price of $35 an ounce. And in his Message to congress of February 6, 1961, the President *pledged that the full strength of our total gold stock and other international reserves stands behind the value of the dollar for use if needed.* [i.e., He pledged all of Fort Knox in supporting this false policy.] The fact that no other countries permit certain private dealings in gold does not clear these inescapable facts." [Editorial comments added.]

Translating the Jargon

In other words, the Treasury Department's answer was simply: we stubbornly stick to the pretense that an ounce of gold is worth only $35 and no more. The rest of the world may not believe this and buy our gold at what they consider to be bargain prices, but unfortunately we can't change foreign laws to outlaw foreigners from owning our gold and calling our bluff. We can, and have, prevented our own citizens from choosing to doubt our assertion that gold is only worth $35 an ounce. We are not about to change that.

The Treasury response also tried to play down fears that foreigners could ever get rid of the paper dollars and claim large amounts of U.S. gold en masse. Foreign-held dollars, Barr said, were only "potential claim[s] against U.S. gold. Certainly, *it is unlikely that all official foreign holders—the only ones eligible to convert dollars into gold for legitimate monetary purposes—would simultaneously request the conversion of their dollars into gold.*" Much like today's banking system, officials are counting on the assumption that everyone will not cash in their chips at the same time.

While "official foreign holders" of dollars (i.e., central banks) may have been the only ones eligible to convert dollars to gold for "legitimate monetary purposes," there is an important fact that Barr evaded. Any individual dealing though a foreign broker could buy U.S. gold by presenting $35 for every ounce. This may have been for an "illegitimate purpose" in Barr's mind, but nevertheless, foreigners (and Americans, operating through foreigners) could buy U.S. gold.

And even though all these people were unlikely to present their dollar to the Treasury simultaneously and thus clean out Fort Knox entirely, he ignored the practical certainty that the volume of claims would continue until, over time, there would be nothing left in Fort Knox. Whether this took ten days or ten years, it was inevitable as long as gold was undervalued.

In the same letter, Barr tried to explain why these claims would never pour in: "The U.S. dollar is after all the major currency for financing trade and payments in the world and is the principal reserve currency of the Free World nations. Working balances are essential to the smooth flow of trade and payments. With our broad and free money markets, dollar reserves can also serve as an income-earning asset by investment in U.S. Treasury or other securities. *In the final analysis, nations retain dollars as part of their international reserves because they have confidence that the value of the dollar will be sustained* and that the United States will impose no restriction on its use. *For these reasons, we have undertaken a wide-ranging balance of payments program designed to bring our accounts ever closer into balance. In this, I am confident, we will—as we must—succeed."*

We now know how wrong these last two forecasts were. The value of the dollar was not sustained, and the payments deficit was not balanced.

Chapter Six

FRANCE STARTS THE COLLAPSE OF THE SYSTEM

On October 19, 1962, Secretary Dillon answered a letter that Representative Henry Gonzalez (D-TX) had written enclosing newspaper clippings charging that there was a run on gold and wanting to know why Washington wasn't concerned. Dillon's reply began:

"First and most important, it is *simply not correct to say that there is a run on our gold.* To be sure, we have continued to lose gold this year, but this outflow is wholly devoid of the atmosphere of rush or panic, which is associated with the term 'run'. Our gold losses are simply the consequence of our balance of payments deficit. As additional dollars come into the hands of foreign monetary authorities, some part of these dollars is converted into gold at the U.S. Treasury, with the exact proportion depending on the laws, traditions and policies of individual foreign countries.

"This is not to deny, of course, that continuing gold losses are a serious problem. Precisely for this reason, the administration has been making a *major and successful effort to curb our balance of payments deficit.* As you know, this deficit was running at the rate of $3.5 billion to $4 billion in each of the three years from 1958 to 1960 but was reduced to $2.5 billion in 1961. We anticipate further substantial progress this year. *As this progress continues, we are confident that the gold outflow will be reduced and eventually eliminated.*"

In other words, 18 months after Kennedy's message, the U.S. was back where it had started: Gold was still leaving the Treasury, and the balance of payments deficit ("additional dollars coming into the hands of" foreigners) was still being blamed. By blaming the payments deficit for the gold outflow, Dillon and Kennedy set up a straw man easy to knock down. Curing the deficit overnight, they said, could be worse than the gold outflow. So they did nothing. As Kennedy put it in his speech to the International Monetary Fund on September 30, 1962:

"The United States could bring its international payments into balance overnight if that were the only goal we sought. We could withdraw our forces, reduce our aid, tie it wholly to purchases in this country, raise high tariff barriers and restrict the foreign investment or other uses of American dollars... such a policy, it is true, would give rise to a new era of dollar shortages, free world insecurity, and American isolation, but we would have 'solved' the balance of payments."

By implication, "solving" the payments deficit would solve the gold outflow but cause worse problems. Blaming the payments deficit for causing the gold outflow was simply a convenient excuse for not taking action to stem the gold outflow. The failure to face the real cause of the outflow ensured that it would continue and accelerate.

What caused the gold outflow was the artificially high value of the dollar and the unrealistically low value placed on gold. Years of inflation had caused the dollar to be worth less. As long as the money managers tried to defy economic reality by claiming the dollar was still worth in gold what it had been before the inflation—as long as they continue blaming inflation's results, instead of its causes—the gold outflow was bound to continue.

What Fiscal Integrity?

On November 24, 1964, New Jersey Senator Clifford Case sent along to Treasury Secretary Dillon this letter written to him by a constituent: "anyone that knows what is going on in Washington knows that today we are on a printing press money economy. The Federal Reserve notes are valueless, there is nothing behind them."

Case asked Secretary Dillon for a response.

On December 3rd, Treasury Undersecretary Roosa wrote, and Dillion signed, a response. The portion quoted here deals with the issue of what backs Federal Reserve Notes:

"Federal Reserve notes, which now constitute 85% of all U.S. money in circulation, are an obligation of the United States and a first lien on all assets of the issuing Federal Reserve Banks. *They are secured by 100% collateral, of which 25% must be in the form of gold certificate reserves.* By law, the *remaining collateral* may consist of U.S. Government securities and eligible short-term paper discounted or purchased by the Federal Reserve System. At present, the collateral is entirely in the form of gold certificates and U.S. Government obligations. However, since gold cannot legally circulate in the United States, the gold reserves held by the Federal Reserve banks are only significant for international settlement. *The real backing behind our currency or that of another country is the fiscal and financial integrity of the government issuing the currency.*"

Let's first take up the statement that Federal Reserve notes "are secured by 100% collateral" including 25% backed by gold. That means that 75% of Federal Reserve Notes were backed by "remaining collateral." What is this? *It turns out to be other government paper promises to pay, either Treasury bills or Treasury bonds.* Dollar bills are promises to pay other promises to pay. Exactly *what* do Treasury bills and bonds promise to pay? More Federal Reserve Notes. We can see why Senator

Case's constituent called Federal Reserve Notes "worthless."

Dillon and Roosa were right, however, when they said that, in the final analysis, without gold the real backing of paper currency is the "fiscal and financial integrity of the government issuing the currency."

Measuring a nation's financial integrity isn't so easy. Fiscal integrity has to do with the income and expenditures of the government, the federal budget. In fiscal year 1964, U.S. government receipts were $89.5 billion. Spending amounted to $97.7 billion. This meant a fiscal budget deficit of about $8 billion. As that time, the total accumulated national debt from 1789 was $313.8 billion.

Skip ahead to today. In fiscal year 2010, revenue was $2.38 trillion. But spending was $3.55 trillion. The budget deficit was $1.17 trillion. This was over 13 times that of 1964's *entire revenue*. On top of that, the total national debt is now well over $14 trillion. Remember that in 1964 the total accumulated national debt from 1789 was only $313.8 billion. This means that the amount of debt piled on since 1964 has increased by nearly 4,500%. This is fiscal integrity?

Another way to measure a country's "financial integrity" is to look at the value of its currency. It took 35 dollars to equal one gold ounce in 1964. Recently it took $1421 to equal that same gold ounce. This is financial integrity?

January 20, 1965—four trucks filled with gold bars estimated to weigh 1.7 million ounces move out of Fort Knox, destined for the railway station at Jeffersonville, Indiana. This is only one of many shipments, which took place during the 1960s as part of official policy. <u>(Reprinted with permission from The Courier-Journal and The Louisville Times)</u>

In 1964, eight U.S. banks failed. At the time of this writing in late 2010, almost 300 banks have failed in the last two years. These days, the list grows longer every Friday. This is financial integrity?

The U.S. fiscal and financial picture in the early 1960s seems healthy to us now. But this health was due to the world's belief that the dollar was fully redeemable, and would remain redeemable in gold. Gold exerts discipline on a government's ability to spend and inflate. Lacking that discipline, or lacking enough gold to enforce that discipline, there are no limits to how much a government can harm its fiscal and financial integrity. And it is clear that the years since the U.S. began dumping its gold have seen a deterioration of the country's fiscal and financial integrity.

By the government's own standards, its policies in the early 1960s failed utterly.

Average Americans should not be lulled into thinking that the question of gold backing the dollar doesn't concern them. It does indeed. Without gold discipline, the government can inflate the money supply and lower the value of the dollar. This makes all things more expensive. That is exactly what has happened since the early 1960s.

It takes more dollars to buy all the things Americans need. Look at housing costs. In the early '60s, it was common to see a man house his family with just 20% of his paycheck and his paycheck alone. Now it is not uncommon to see housing costs take up 40%-50% of the income in a household where both husband and wife are working.

By this most basic measure, we can see how anti-gold policies of the 1960s have created an environment in which the average American's standard of living has declined. You don't need me to tell you that in recent years the rich have gotten richer, the poor have gotten poorer, and the middle class is vanishing.

But just to keep this story to gold and Federal Reserve policies, think about how things would have been different for housing if gold had been a disicpline on the Fed. In the early 2000s, the Fed put interest rates down to near zero. This caused banks to lend money to nearly anyone with a pulse, and the money went into real estate. Property prices zoomed and created a bubble. That bubble burst around 2007 and we will be feeling the effects of this for years to come. Had a form of gold standard been in the system, the Fed would not have been able to lower interest rates to such artificially and ultimately dangerously low levels, setting off the largest real estate boom and now bust in history.

France Balks

Even while America was losing her gold during the early 1960s, the issue played no part in the 1964 U.S. presidential election. As far as the American people were concerned, there was no problem when Lyndon Johnson began his term of office on January 20, 1965. By the end of his term, the whole Gold Pool would collapse amidst chaos. But few would have predicted it that day.

This brief calm was shattered two weeks later. The most powerful voice yet raised attacked the $35 fixed price concept. On February 4, 1965,

French President Charles de Gaulle held a press conference urging a return to the gold standard. Inherent in his proposal was an abondonment of the fixed $35 price and an increase in the dollar price of gold.

Ironically, this attack on the unrealistically fixed $35 price came from the nation that had benefited the most from it. During the Gold Pool years (1961-68), the Bank of France purchased more official $35 gold than any other central bank. Table C shows that the French government took almost 65 million ounces, nearly twice that of second-place Britain.

TABLE C

United States Monetary Gold Transactions 1961-1968

Recipient Country	Dollars (Million)	Fine Troy Ounces (Million)
France	2,267.1	64.77
United Kingdom	1,230.0	35.14
Spain	644.3	18.41
Japan and other Asian Countries	440.0	12.57
Austria	405.0	11.57
Belgium	388.2	11.09
Germany (West)	247.5	7.07
Africa	242.0	6.91
Switzerland	236.0	6.74
Netherlands	138.9	3.97
Italy	134.0	3.83

The French had long been believers in gold. They had seen their paper currencies collapse to worthlessness too many times in their history to hold any illusion about the value of paper money that lacked gold backing.

Hours after de Gaulle's press conference, the U.S. Treasury put out the three-paragraph response to it:

Washington, DC
February 4, 1965

President de Gaulle has recommended that the gold exchange standard, based on the use of dollars freely convertible into gold at $35 an ounce, and which has served the world well for 30 years be abandoned. He has proposed that instead we retreat to the full gold standard which collapsed in 1931 and which proved incapable of financing the huge increase of world trade that has marked the twentieth century.

Studies of possible ways to improve the world monetary system have been underway for the past 18 months in the International Monetary Fund and in the Group of ten countries making up the GAB. The new French proposals will presumably be introduced in these forums where a number of other proposals have been under study for some time. However, a move toward the restoration of the so-called gold standard, with all its rigidities and sharp deflationary consequences, would be quite contrary to the main stream of thinking among the governments participating in these studies.

In no event would any solution be acceptable that involved a change in the fixed $35 price of gold. It is also essential that any changes in the system ensure that adequate international credit will continue to be available to finance the swings in trade typical of a growing world economy.

The emphasized sentence in the Treasury release sums it all up: The U.S. government was not going to change the overvalued dollar price of gold either to satisfy France or to reflect reality.

Chapter Seven

ROOSA'S SPEECH

Three months after de Gaulle's announcement, Monetary Undersecretary Robert Roosa gave a most complete explanation and defense of U.S. policy at the Council on Foreign Relations in New York City on May 10, 1965, Roosa delivered a talk entitled "The Conditions for Monetary Order."

Before exploring such touchy areas as gold, Roosa first outlined six points so "above controversy... that their...acceptance will be presumed, not debated." While each point had its importance, we will focus on Number 4:

"4. The monetary authorities of most countries will maintain reserves in the form of widely acceptable liquid assets. Because gold has been tested as a store of value through the centuries, while man-made monies have suffered violent changes, most counties will wish to include some gold in their reserves. They will also wish to be assured that other liquid assets which they hold are readily convertible into gold. They look upon gold convertibility as an assurance that the value of any other asset, accepted as a substitute for gold, will be kept reasonably stable. They need an anchor of stability to help in checking the inherent pressures for excess that are generated by expanding economies."

Roosa's fourth point is a good defense of gold. People do need currency stability, and "man-made monies" have historically not provided it for long. But Roosa thought that **his** man-made money would be different. He valued the dollar more highly than gold, and he viewed America's role as the world's banker the way, in 1965, others regarded it as the world's policeman. In other words, he lost sight of the fact that, even in 1965—at the peak of U.S. power—there were limits to what the U.S. could do. It could not, for instance, wave a magic wand and turn unlimited supplies of paper money into gold.

And yet that, in essence, is what he spent much of his talk trying to do, defending both the $35 gold fixing and America's role as the world's banker: "there are, in addition, other characteristics of the present system that seem to me to be equally essential for the future. One is that the United States must itself maintain the $35 price for gold. A second is that the United States must continue to serve as a banker for the world, with the dollar in widespread use both as a vehicle currency and also, at least on the present scale, as a reserve currency."

Stability Over Reality

Then came his defense of the fixed $35 price:

"The gold-dollar has become the central influence for stability throughout the postwar period. Country after country, after suffering the effects at home and abroad of an erratic but continuing deterioration in the value of its own currency, has made a new start toward stability by defining the par value of its currency in terms of the dollar, a dollar whose convertibility into gold at an unvarying price has remained assured. The fact and the example of that certainty have been intangible but powerful forces in enabling other countries to press for stability in their own monetary affairs. In turn, the wish of each country to earn dollars, and to use them, has created a new environment of effective but not rigid accommodation to the necessities of balance of payments discipline. For these other countries found linked with this currency of relatively stable value, that was convertible on demand into gold at a fixed price, an array of credit facilities that enabled their traders, bankers, and governments to supplement their operating balances or their monetary reserves through borrowing in the United States, and to earn interest on balances held in the United States. The dollar became the center of a system that was much more flexible, and much more capable of responding to shifting needs, than any system based upon gold alone. At its fixed $35 price in terms of gold, the dollar has itself become a tradition. Much of the confidence now gained by many other currencies throughout the world is in turn rooted in that tradition."

A paper money-based system is indeed more "flexible" and "capable of responding to shifting needs." But these "needs" are the needs of governments to inflate when they feel they need to, to manipulate their currencies when they want to; in short, to create instant wealth without having to produce it. This has been the dream of every government that has tried to substitute its man-made monetary values for gold's natural ones. In that sense, a truly adhered-to gold system is inflexible: It does not allow governments to manipulate and destroy the value of people's money.

Roosa's talk of the dollar being a "tradition" is a prime example of the delusion of grandeur monetary officials have always had when they confuse *the symbol* with *the substance behind the symbol.* (The dollar began in 1792 only as a convenient way to carry the gold or silver it was backed by; it had no value in itself.) This confusion causes the symbol—in this case the dollar—sooner or later to become completely unglued from the substance behind it, and any "tradition" to vanish. Indeed, a mere six years after Roosa spoke these words, the tradition was over.

Government's Excuse for Dumping Gold

Roosa then provided the government's official excuse for dumping the people's gold to prop up the dollar:

"It has been recognition of the overriding importance of the dollar, both as vehicle currency and a reserve currency for much of the world, that has motivated successive Presidents of the United States to *renew the assurance that the $35 price would be defended with all necessary means; that the price would, in fact, be immutable. To withdraw that pledge would, in itself, shatter the structure of confidence which has supported the most remarkable expansion of trade among nations in the history of the world*—an expansion in which the United States itself has fully shared, and from which its own standard of living has amply gained."

Roosa also brought up a more practical argument against devaluing the dollar, which, on the face of it, is plausible:

"Moreover, if one were to be so cynical or so theoretically inclined as to ignore the obligations which the United States has accepted, there are also compelling if more earthy reasons for maintaining the fixed price. One is that the United States, by virtue of its immense size within the trading markets of the world, cannot for the foreseeable future expect to be able to exercise an independent judgment in determining its own exchange rate vis-à-vis the rest of the world. Any attempt to devalue the dollar by writing up the price of gold would assuredly be matched, within hours, by comparable and offsetting action on the part of virtually every other country. The United States would be foreclosed by its size, if it were not already prevented by its committed obligations, from unilateral devaluation. Thus, unable to change its parity against other countries, *the United States would find that all that would result from a change in the price of gold would be the indicated profit from the mark-up on whatever was the stock of gold held at the time by the United States.*

"The act of repudiation, and the subsequent spreading of distrust in dollar obligations, would surely lead many monetary authorities to convert the dollars still held in their monetary reserves into gold. Indeed, some who have argued for a change in the dollar price of gold have also suggested that the United States should in any event distribute to other official holders an amount of gold (or an equivalent in added dollars) sufficient to compensate for the loss they would have incurred on dollars held at the time of an upward change in the gold price. *Whichever the course, the United States would very likely soon be left with no more gold, at the new inflated price, than it had held before the price change occurred. Quite probably, its remaining holdings even valued at the new higher gold price, would be far less."*

This did indeed raise a good point. An increase in the price for which America will sell its gold would not by itself solve the problem. If the U.S. government did not begin living within its means and stop inflating it would only be a matter of time before it would face the problem again. If the government put the price much higher than the market price, as

Roosevelt did in 1934, gold holders would happily sell gold to the Treasury, as they did in 1934.

While this would buy time, it would not be a permanent solution to the government's temptation to inflate. Indeed, with so much gold locked up, there would be perhaps even more temptation to inflate, as in the 1930s. And the very act of inflation causes distortions in the economy too numerous to documents here. *The only real recipe for long-term currency stability is to take the power to inflate away from the world's central banks by making them adhere to a fixed rate at which all people— domestically and abroad—can claim gold by turning in paper.* A run on gold would result if the government printed too many paper claims on that gold. This run would force the government to live within its means.

Preventing "Widely Fluctuating Exchange Rates"

By the time Roosa gave his speech in 1965, his flawed system was facing real problems. But this is how he answered those who wanted to prevent all gold from leaving the country:

"To all of this, the answer has been given that the United States should instead simply place an embargo on all sales of gold and establish no selling price. In such circumstances, however, the United States would have to buy or sell other currencies in order to maintain the relations which its trade required with other countries. It would be left then in a position of continual jockeying over the appropriate exchange rate with every other country."

In other words, without a fixed definition of what a dollar is worth, the dollar could be traded, and accounts only be settled, by constantly attempting to define what the dollar is worth in terms of every other country. This would be a system of, as he puts it in the next sentence, "widely fluctuating exchange rates." Well, since the gold-exchange system collapsed in 1973, we have had just that: a system of widely fluctuating exchange rates.

From 1973 to 1979 the yen doubled against the dollar. From 1979 to 1985 the dollar doubled against the yen. And from 1985 to 1995 the yen almost tripled against the dollar. Within three years after that, by 1998, it had plunged in half against the dollar. Then in the two years following that, it doubled. Over the next two years (2000-2002), the yen sank 25%. Since then, it has soared to, as I write, 15-year highs. What could be more "widely fluctuating" than *that*?

Through it all, the world economy has adjusted in its own fashion. Governments, however, still waste millions of dollars of taxpayers' money in trying to artificially support or depress currency values that the market has decided should go otherwise. These expenditures are actually huge subsidies to big banks and astute currency speculators around the world. Like those who bet against the U.S.

ability to successfully defend an artificially high dollar and low gold price, these men essentially take money from the taxpayers of all the nations whose governments intervene in currency markets to manipulate their monies.

Later in his 1965 talk, Roosa criticized floating exchange rates. He rightly defended the need for stability in the monetary system, which in fact has been absent in the currency chaos since 1973. "[M]ost governments have recognized the over-riding need for a reasonably stable unit of measurement. Governments know, too, that their traders cannot function as well...when the normal range of credit risks...is enlarged several times over by uncertainty as to the amount of their own currency which they will actually pay, or receive, when any given transaction is finally consummated. Only situations with very high profits margins, capable of covering these extra risks, will seem attractive. Total world trade will, as a result, be held down. Whether the risk is carried by the trader himself, or shifted by the trader to the futures market (in the case of those currencies for which an active futures market might exist), the over-ride in cost would necessarily make many transactions prohibitive.

"By contrast, a system of fixed rates, hinged as the present system is to a strong center currency, and in turn to gold, has its clear reference points. A country hat is slipping behind sees the impact, to be sure, in downward pressure on its exchange rate."

In other words, according to this argument, under fixed rates with set currency values, a country which inflates too much will suffer a run on its exchange rate and be forced to devalue. This public admission of sin will keep nations on the straight and narrow.

But what happens when the "strong center currency" itself inflates? Then that nation risks a run on its gold until it too devalues. But devaluation is just what Roosa and the rest of the government refused to do! Without that devaluation, without an end to the inflation and finally, without an embargo on gold shipments, gold was inevitably going to continue to flow out of the country. Why these bright men apparently did not realize what to us seems obvious is another unanswered question in our story.

The World's Banker

Roosa ended his defense of the gold giveaway by describing America as a country that for "...compelling reasons, *stands ready at all times to sell gold in unlimited quantities at the $35 price...*

"One final reason for maintaining the existing United States position, in buying and selling gold at the $35 price, is the reinforcement that this gives to the continued role fulfilled by the United States as principal banker for the world.

"It has been increasingly common for people in this country to comment, sometimes irritably if not petulantly, that the time has come for the United States to give up its role as world banker. What is it, after all, the question goes, that the United States gets from being a reserve currency center, other than severe criticism from abroad and exposure to demands from others for the gold in our own reserves?"

Good question, Mr. Roosa. What did the United States get in exchange for letting so much of its gold go?

The only concrete answer Roosa could give was that the "United States [has been] able as a nation to gain through the income received in performing financial services…"

But this income—whatever it was—could not prevent a balance of payments deficit.

Looking back from a vantage point of half a century, it is hard to see just that the U.S. got out of this arrangement except the right to call itself the world's banker. But it was an expensive privilege, and one that wiped out almost 60% of the nation's gold reserves and made a return to a genuine gold standard much more difficult and painful.

We are now paying the price for those years of official self-delusion. Instead of unquestioned superiority, our too-expensive global commitments have instead made us dangerously dependent on foreign bankers and capital. And as America mindlessly borrows foreign capital to pay for— and prop up—an overextended empire, less encumbered nations like China, Japan, Germany, and Korea are overtaking us industrially.

This, then, is the result of the policy that during the early 1960s tried to reorder the monetary world by defying age-old economic reality.

Chapter Eight

THE FINAL COLLAPSE

When Roosa spoke, there were only a few more months of strength left to the system he tried to defend. In 1966, the unraveling accelerated.

In August of that year, France began buying gold for its own account and not for the London Gold Pool. By the end of 1966, France had purchased $601 million of gold (about 17.2 million ounces). Total U.S. sales to all foreign countries that year was $608 million (the U.S. also bought nearly $200 million worth of gold, much of it from Canada, so its net loss to foreign countries was "only" $431 million, or 12.3 million ounces) when you add sales to the Gold Pool and domestic producers or consumers, *the total U.S. official gold loss in 1966 was 16.3 million ounces.*

In 1967, the total loss was 33.4 million ounces, or 1.17 billion badly overvalued dollars. Over 80% of this gold went to Great Britain in a futile attempt to save the pound from devaluation. By 1967's end, the total U.S. gold stock stood at 345 million ounces, less than *half* the total at the 1949 peak. More important to officials though, was that the total gold store was quickly shrinking toward the 25% legal minimum backing for the paper money.

By early 1968 the U.S. faced a stark choice: either eliminate the legal requirement that there be a 25% gold "cover" for the domestic money supply, or soon have no more gold left to "defend" the dollar. The decision they reached comes as no surprise: the 25% requirement was repealed, with almost no debate, in March 1968.

This was the final attempt to keep the Pool going. By eliminating all legal reason to hold any gold, the Johnson administration announced that all U.S. gold would be disposable for "international purposes." The U.S. government tried to get its allies to keep dumping gold as well. But by that time the six other nations had had enough. France had dropped out of the Pool in 1967, and the U.S. had taken over France's 9% share of the Pool. But when the others decided to follow France out, the U.S. clearly had to throw in the towel. Even American officials realized that they alone could not keep selling gold at the $35 price to all comers. The London Gold Pool was allowed to lapse. Ironically, this happened one day after the bill abolishing the 25% gold cover and "freeing" all U.S. gold became law.

(NOTE TO CREATESPACE: Please place Table D on own page.)

TABLE D

U.S. Net Monetary Gold Transactions with Foreign Countries and International and Regional Organizations (In millions of dollars at $35 per fine troy ounce; negative figures represent net sales by the United States; positive figures, net acquisitions)

Area and Country	Calendar Year					1970		1971		
	1966	1967	1968	1969	1970[1]	Jul-Sep	Oct-Dec[1]	Jan-Mar	Apr-Jun	Jul-Sep
Western Europe:										
Austria	-25			4						
Belgium			-58						-110	
Denmark	-13			25	-2	-2				
France	-601		600	325	-129		-129		-282	-191
Germany				500						
Greece	-1	19	-11	-1	-10		-10			
Italy	-60	-85	-209	-76						
Netherlands			-19		-50	-20	-30	-25		
Spain					51	51				
Switzerland	-2	-30	-50	-25	-50	-50		-75	-50	-50
Turkey	-12	*	3	-18	1	-5	9	15	-3	
United Kingdom	80	-879	-835							
Bank Int'l Settlements				200						
Other	-23	-3	-90	36	-15	-1	-21	*	-3	-22
Total Western Europe	**-659**	**-980**	**-669**	**969**	**-204**	**-27**	**-180**	**-85**	**-448**	**-263**
Canada	200	150	50							

Latin American Republics:										
Argentina	-39	-1	-25	-25	-28		-23			
Brazil	-3	-1	*		-23		-23			
Colombia	7	*		*	-1					
Mexico	10	-10			-25		-25			
Peru		35		-12	-13	-3	-10	*	-4	
Venezuela										
Other	-16	-14	-40	-18	-42	-1	-31	*	*	*
Total Latin America	**-41**	**9**	**-65**	**-54**	**-131**	**-4**	**-111**	*	**-4**	*

Asia:										
Japan	-56				-119		-119			
Other	-30	-44	-366	42	-95	-39	-79	-15	10	-32
Total Asia	**-86**	**-44**	**-366**	**42**	**-213**	**-39**	**-197**	**-15**	**10**	**-32**

Africa:

Total Africa	-19	-157	-66	-9	-70	-4	-64	-1	-2	*

Other Countries:

Total Other Countries	-3	-9	-2	9	-11		-11		-2	

Total Foreign Countries	-608	-1031	-1118	957	-631	-73	-563	-102	-445	-296

International & regional organizations[2]	177	22	-3	10	-156	-322	142	-7	-11	-4

Grand total	-431	-1009	-1121	967	-787[1]	-395	-422[1]	-109	-457	-300

[1] Includes in 1970 total (Oct-Dec 1970) the U.S. payment of $385 million increase in its gold subscription to the IMF and gold sold by the IMF to the United States in mitigation of U.S. sales to other countries making gold payments to the IMF. The country data include, for the same period, gold sales by the United States to various countries in connection with IMF quota payments. Such sales to countries and resales by the IMF totaled $548 million each.

[2] Includes International Monetary Fund gold sales to and purchases from the United States, gold deposits by the IMF and withdrawal of deposits. The first withdrawal, amounting to $17 million, was made in June 1968.

*Less than $500,000.

The U.S. Treasury then tried a different tack: they announced that private parties could no longer buy Fort Knox gold. Only requests from foreign governments would be honored.

After 1968's huge loss (33.5 million ounces shipped out) this strategy seemed to work. In 1969, due in large part to Treasury gold purchases from Germany, total U.S. gold stock rose by 27.6 million ounces. It was the first increase since 1957, before the gold rush started.

While this calmed people, the problems were not yet over. Continued inflation of the paper money supply caused renewed pressures on America's gold. Even though only foreign governments were buying, they were buying. In 1970, purchases by the governments of France, Switzerland, and Japan helped clear out 22.5 million ounces. Moreover, as table D shows, the trend worsened as the year wore on. As the fateful year 1971 began, so did renewed buying. Sales accelerated, and by mid-summer America's policymakers realized that at the rate things were going, as much as 20% of what remained in Fort Knox would be cleaned out by year's end. Everyone admitted this couldn't continue.

Therefore, on August 15, 1971 President Nixon ended the whole charade. He decreed that no more gold would be released to anyone from Fort Knox in exchange for dollars. He closed the "gold window" and officially ended what, by then, had become a grand fiction: that the dollar was as "good as gold." On December 17, he devalued the dollar by 8.5%. But it was an odd act: $38 per ounce became the new gold price, but a price at which the U.S. would not sell gold.

There was one exception: the International Monetary Fund. As part of America's obligation to contribute to a fund which would make loans to nations in deep financial trouble, a final 15.5 million ounces left U.S. government hands in 1972.

That ended it. The damage had been done.

The Questions Begin

When Nixon finally closed the gold window, the massive flow of gold out of the treasury halted. But look where it left us: By the end of 1972, only 276 million ounces were left, compared to 653 million ounces of official U.S. gold in 1957. In just 15 years, 377 million ounces, nearly 58% of the supply had gone. At today's price of $1400 per ounce, that's a loss of over half a trillion dollars.

And, for what purpose, we must ask? To support a policy that ended in failure. No nation can endlessly print paper currency and expect it to hold its value against gold, or any other material asset of finite amount. The more dollars there are in existence, the less value each one has. The Federal Reserve can double the amount of dollars in existence, but then it will take about twice the dollars it did to buy an ounce of gold.

The Treasury should have realized this fact in the 1960s. Had they raised the dollar price of gold to a level reflecting the amount of dollars the Federal Reserve System had created, the gold outflow would have stopped.

But even that would not have done any lasting good as long as the government continued to spend money beyond its means to pay for it, and to print money to make up the difference.

The fact is that the hard choices were not made and over half the nation's gold was allowed to leave the country in the interest of a policy that tried to deny reality.

We have the right to raise some questions about this. Anyone would. For instance, did these officials from four administrations violate their fiduciary duty by letting over half the gold leave Fort Knox from 1958 to 1972?

From our perspective today, the answer is surely yes. Regardless of whether they believed they were doing the right thing, we now realize that by imprudently allowing so much gold to leave government hands they were doing great harm to our economy. The years from the late 1950s through the early 1970s directly preceded a period—from 1973 to the present—when American standards of living have been steadily falling.

It is reasonable to charge that the mistakes of the 15 years before 1973 directly caused the American economy to slip in the years since then.

Kennedy said the government was willing to defend the dollar's value using any weapon—including gold—at its disposal. But we should ask the economic policymakers of that 15-year period whether or not they succeeded. Has the dollar's value been maintained? Sadly, the answer is surely no.

How Much Did We Lose?

By just how much did the government fail to keep the dollar stable? There are many ways of gauging the value of the dollar. The house across the street from me sold for $17,000 in 1963. Without any additions, it sold for $220,000 in 1987. By that measure, the dollar had lost a whopping 92% of its 1963 value.

I don't need to tell you that any house which sold for $220,000 in 1987 would sell for much more in 2011. In fact, 2 years ago that house sold for $910,000. Thus, in what the dollar can buy in housing, it has lost over 98%. Even accounting for the general fall in housing prices since 2008 —say it now would sell for only $750,00, it is safe to say the dollar has lost over 97% of its value.

But let's take a more universal tangible asset, one which we've been talking about. Gold's price was $35 in 1961 (and 1971, for that matter). Today, the price hovers around $1,400 dollars. This means what took $35 to buy in 1971 now takes $1,400. In easier terms, what cost one dollar then now costs $40. By this measure, the dollar has lost almost exactly the same amount of its value—over 97%— against the universal measure of gold as it did against the house on my street.

Any way you slice it, the dollar's value is only a shadow of what it was when Kennedy publicly pledged our gold to keep the dollar stable. We`ve lost most of our gold. Gold is the only real discipline on the ability of the government to spend and inflate, and inflation causes the value of the dollar to deteriorate. Therefore, the absence of gold to back the currency can be seen to have made inflation easier. And inflation has caused living standards to fall. Today, everyone in the family has to work to afford the things that only one head of a household could buy with one job in the 1950s and '60s.

That is why this issue affects everyone. And that is why the questions should be asked.

Part III

Chapter Nine

QUESTIONS OPEN THE VAULT AT FORT KNOX

Questions such as these caused private citizens to pester politicians and bureaucrats in Washington about a number of policies relating to gold. This set off a chain of events that culminated in a plan to allow elected representatives into Fort Knox for the first time since Roosevelt visited the depository in 1943.

One such question came in an August 1974 exchange of correspondence between Attorney General William Saxbe and a longtime acquaintance and financial supporter of his Ohio congressional campaigns named Edward Durell.

Durell pointed out to his old acquaintance that the Nixon administration and many of its officials had recently been forced out of office and accused of perjury, misuse of power, and obstruction of justice. If these men had been at the head of a company, new management coming in would naturally want to check the inventory of valuables, especially "high dollar items," to make sure all was in order. Therefore, he urged a complete physical inventory of the nation's gold by a top-notch independent auditing firm.

Durell also wanted to know exactly how many gold bars were of "good delivery" quality; i.e. of a quality that is accepted on world markets. (There is no such thing as a bar of "pure gold." There is always some alloy in fabricated gold.) Bars made up of .995 fine gold or better are considered "good delivery" gold.

Another question addressed how long it had been since the bars had been counted, weighed and assayed. (Assaying means determining the fineness of the bar.)

Saxbe's letter contained several notable comments: "... the Director of the Mint appoints annual settlement committees to take a physical inventory of the assets at the coinage mints, assay offices, and bullion depositories . . .the members of the committee verify the amount of all gold not under seal and inspect all joint seals attached to sealed compartments to ensure that the seals have not been disturbed and the contents remain intact. . . . Given these procedures, there is simply no reasonable possibility that there is any truth whatsoever to the allegations that gold was unlawfully removed from the U.S. gold stock. . . ."

Once again, the government's response raised more questions than it answered. The seals on sealed compartments in Fort Knox are checked to see that they haven't been broken. But the gold inside is not actually counted—it's not even looked at to make sure the compartment actually contains gold. The gold not under seal is "verified".

But what does "verified" mean? How long has it been since all the bars have been counted, weighed or assayed? As long as the seals are still intact, the compartments are not opened. And finally, what about the questions regarding the quality of the gold in Fort Knox? The issue is never even addressed. Almost as if they knew their answers were inadequate, Treasury officials "extended an open invitation," Saxbe told Durell, "to all members of the Banking and Currency Committee of the U.S. House of Representatives to conduct a personal inspection of Fort Knox or any other gold depository."

The Vault Opens—or Does It?

The following month, on September 23, 1974, Mary Brooks, Director of the U.S. Mint, led six congressmen and one senator on a tour of Fort Knox. It was the first time since Roosevelt visited on April 28, 1943 that anyone except Mint and Treasury employees had been allowed inside.

This tour evidently resulted from the spate of printed allegations which appeared earlier that year. Representative Philip Crane (R-Ill) in July personally brought these allegations to the attention of Treasury

Secretary William Simon. And Simon apparently gave the order to allow the tour.

The whole tour lasted less than four hours, and the visitors were plainly shown only what the Treasury officials intended they should see. The entire atmosphere was carnival-like, and only one of the thirteen compartments supposed to contain gold was actually opened to the visitors. They were also shown bars that were orangish in hue, and it was later revealed that these particular bars were only about 90% gold and 10% copper. (The pre-1933 gold coins from which these bars came were themselves nearly 10% copper.) This is not good delivery gold.

Mrs. Mary Brooks, Director of the Mint, displays a vault filled with gold bars on the occasion of an inspection by members of Congress September 23, 1974. (Photo by AP/Wide World Photos).

Fort Knox tour, September 24, 1°974. Rep. John B. Conlan (R-Ariz.) weighs a bar of gold from the vault opened to the visitors. Seen members of Congress toured the depository at an inspection directed by Mrs. Mary Brooks, Director of the Mint.
(AP/Wide World Photos)

All of the congressional visitors pronounced themselves satisfied that "all the gold" was there. But there was no way they could prove this. In fact, this tour failed to put to rest outside doubts; if anything, the doubts increased.

This brings up some of the unusual aspects of our whole story. The Treasury must bear responsibility for the fact that many doubts and questions still remain. The tour itself was a tacit admission by Treasury that there were questions to answer. But the half-measure means by which it chose to answer those questions suggested that the Treasury was reluctant to take full measures to allay all doubts, because it was afraid of what might be revealed.

The frivolous atmosphere of the visit to Fort Knox gave encouragement to those who believed the Treasury was not telling the full story and had something to hide.

The Audit of the Gold Reserves

The same might be said for the audit of the gold supplies which began the day after the tour. Also meant as a gesture to quell doubts, it did nothing of the sort. The Treasury agreed to audit 20% of the stock over a 30-day period to begin September 24, 1974. This, however, was another case of admitting a response should be made, but then failing to respond fully enough to satisfy all doubters.

There were enough complaints, in fact, to convince the Treasury in late 1974 to agree to audit all the remaining stock. Again, officials chose to proceed in a way which could not eliminate reasonable doubt. They decided to audit 10% of the remaining gold every year for 10 years until all was audited.

One Step Ahead

There are documented cases in 19th century California history of crooked bankers who, upon having their branches audited one by one, were able to stretch out the travel time of the auditors between branches so that, by means of a faster horse, gold previously counted could be sent ahead to the next bank with the auditors unaware they had seen the same gold before. The possibility of something like this occurred to the doubters, when they heard of this 10% per year scheme. Surely a plan like this would allow ample time for funny business, they reasoned.

Aggravating these citizens' fear was the fact that the government itself was carrying out the audit. It is common practice for shareholders of a company under audit to demand that the audit be done by an independent company. Why, then, the doubters reasoned, shouldn't the government hire one of the Big Eight accounting firms to come in and do the job?

Further, the Treasury audit was not a physical inventory of the number and quality of each gold bar. The wax seals on the unopened compartments were checked. Only a few were opened, and of those, only spot check counts were made. Of those counted, only a few bars were weighed, and of those, only a few assayed.

Both the Fort Knox tour and the subsequent audit failed to quell the questions and, in fact, served only to raise so many more concerns that, by early 1976, one of the six congressmen who had taken the tour, John Conlan (R-AZ), wrote Secretary Simon:

"I am not satisfied that the questions have been adequately answered. To some extent Government response to legitimate questions has exacerbated the gold controversy and added to suspicions that something is awry in this matter."

Ten Percent Good Delivery Gold

After the results of the audit were issued in February 1975, Edward Durell (whose letters to Saxbe had received unsatisfactory answers the year before) made it clear to his congressman, J. Kenneth Robinson (R-VA), that he wasn't pleased by the nature of the government's 30-day audit.

As a result of Robinson's subsequent actions, the General Accounting Office (GAO) first sent two men to Robinson's office, then four men to Durell's Virginia farm in attempts to defend their accounting practices. In charge was Hyman Krieger, the Washington regional manager of the GAO.

One concrete piece of information to come out of this meeting was Krieger's admission that only a small part—24.4 million ounces—of the official gold was of a quality .995 fine or better. That is, *less than 10% of the 264 million ounces held by the Treasury could be considered good delivery gold.* Krieger confirmed this in a letter to Durell of April 11, 1975:

"We analyzed, as agreed, the gold bar schedules for Fort Knox and found that fine gold in good delivery form (.995 or better) at Fort Knox totaled 24,411,140 ounces."

Mr. Krieger further referred to differences in what is considered "good delivery gold". As you can see from the pictures of gold bars in this book, gold sellers compete amongst themselves to provide gold of a fineness of .9999 or "Four Nines". Indeed, some gold, such as some issues of the Canadian Maple Leaf coin, is sold in purity of "Five Nines" or .99999 fine. In the international gold market, there is a minimum standard of .9995 fineness for gold to truly be considered "good delivery". But Krieger says in the letter that "The Treasury Department stated (and we have seen nothing to the contrary) that a fineness factor of only .995 or better meets this [good delivery] standard. You might be interested to know that 16,937,189 ounces do meet a .9995 standard of fineness".

Think of it: He's essentially saying that out of the 262 million ounces of gold that officially comprises America's gold stock, just under 17 million meet what in the real world is considered the bare minimum standard of good delivery purity.

Neither Treaury nor Kreiger made any reference to the purity of the rest of the gold other than the fact that it doesn't even measure up to their low standard of .995 fine. We know that this other 90 plus percent is not good delivery gold, we just don't know how bad the quality is.

But at least one of the questions which had been raised was answered completely by this face-to-face visit with the GAO. Unfortunately, the answer served only to confirm the worst fears: Not only did we lose more than 60% of our good delivery gold, 90% of what remains is coin melt. (It's generally accepted that the gold which left Fort Knox was good delivery gold—certainly foreign governments and banks would have accepted nothing less.) This cannot be counted as a part of the U.S. reserves because the confiscation of privately owned gold in 1933 has never been upheld by the Supreme Court; and many experts in constitutional law believe it was clearly unconstitutional. This means that the coin melt gold probably belongs to the American people, as private citizens, and not the government. And that means that only 25 million ounces of gold are left in the official U.S. gold stock. Thus, the government has given away almost *all* its gold.

Chapter Ten

SIMON'S BEST RESPONSE

The September 1974 congressional tour of Fort Knox did not stop the inquiries. All through 1975 and early 1976, questions were put to Treasury officials by various congressmen, some of which were answered one by one. Finally, the Treasury apparently decided to tie together all the official responses in one place. This decision resulted in a memorandum prepared in the spring of 1976, 18 months after the October 1974 Fort Knox tour. As far as I am aware, the Treasury Department is still using this memorandum.

It is interesting to discover how this response came about. In early 1976, Representative John Conlan of Arizona wrote to Treasury Secretary William Simon. One year earlier Conlan had been one of the six congressmen allowed to "peep" into one of the Fort Knox vaults. At the time, he pronounced himself satisfied. However, 14 months later he had second thoughts. Specifically, he wasn't satisfied that the gold was of the quality the Treasury claimed.

The first three paragraphs of Conlan's February 26, 1976 letter to Simon read as follows:

"Dear Bill,

As you know, controversy over the quantity and fineness of U.S. gold holdings at Fort Knox and other depositories has continued for several years. Well-regarded citizens and members of the news media have joined in asking serious questions about the factual situation concerning the total stock of U.S. gold bullion and international transactions involving U.S. gold.

I am not satisfied that the questions have been adequately answered. To some extent, government response to legitimate questions has exacerbated the gold controversy and added to suspicions that something is awry in this matter. Certainly a final determination of the total factual situation is long past due.

I would urge you to order a full-scale inventory of all gold holdings at our several depositories. This would hopefully include the necessary mechanical tests and other accounting to document the fineness of all U.S. gold bullion at each location, and to satisfy Congress and the general public that no U.S. gold is missing or has been illegally used or transferred for the benefit of any person, organization or nation. Such a complete inventory of U.S. gold holdings has not been conducted since 1954 [sic]."

Of course we know that the 1953 audit was not really worthy of the name.

Conlan's letter received a response from Secretary Simon on May 4, 1976. Simon's last line explained why he didn't want a complete audit: "[It] would be a very costly undertaking and an unnecessary expense to the taxpayers."

Simon also enclosed a memorandum which, more completely than anything before or since, raises some of the allegations of the doubters and seeks to answer them. This very interesting document was prepared by the Department of the Treasury to give "the factual reply to each allegation" raised by the news media and private citizens.

Allegations and Responses

[Note: Most of these allegations are quoted verbatim by the Treasury from correspondence or news articles.]

Allegation # 1		Treasury's Response
"In 1954, the depository at Fort Knox contained some 715 million ounces of gold. Today [in 1976] it has only 147 million ounces according to Government figures. Missing is an estimated 568 million ounces of gold valued at almost $90 billion on today's open market."		Gold holdings at Fort Knox on January 1, 1954 were 356.7 million ounces, not 715 million. Holdings on December 31, 1975 were 147.4 million ounces. A total of 209.3 million ounces was withdrawn between January 1, 1954 and December 31, 1975. All of the sixteen withdrawals took place between

		1962 and 1971: 185.7 million ounces were shipped to the U.S. Assay Office in New York, 9.3 million ounces to the Federal Reserve Bank of New York and 14.3 million ounces to the Bank of England in London. Details of each of these withdrawals have been made public.

Comment: This is an example of the Tresury setting up a "straw man" and easily knocking it down. The main point raised by critics was not that gold had left *Fort Knox,* but that gold from the *entire reserves* left this country as a part of official U.S. policy. Treasury's own published figures show that total gold stores were reduced from 701 million ounces in 1949 to 276 million ounces in 1973. The Treasury officials attempted to minimize the loss by focusing on only one depository. However, while the *withdrawals* from depositories is documented, as we will see, exact details about where the gold *went* were not forthcoming, even after much effort.

Allegation # 2		Treasury's Response
"Officials of the U.S. Bureau of the Mint and U.S. Treasury Department have told conflicting stories on the movement of the nation's gold reserves and in some instances have blatantly lied about gold shipments—for example, [outside] investigators learned		When the U.S. Government was engaged in the purchase and sale of gold, the transactions were normally handled through the Assay Office or the Federal Reserve Bank of New York. Gold was shipped from Fort Knox as needed to maintain s

| that during a two-month period in late 1967 billions of dollars worth of U.S. gold were flown into England". | | an appropriate supply at the Assay Office and Reserve Bank. However, these shipments did not necessarily reflect a reduction in the total U.S. gold stock. The attached table summariethe changes in the total U.S.A gold stock between December 31, 1953 and December 31, 1975. |

TABLE E

Sources: Federal Reserve Bulletin, Annual Report of the Director of the Mint, U.S. Department of the Treasury, March 24, 1976

Analysis of Net Changes in U.S. Gold Stock 1954-1975 (millions of ounces)

Gold Stock	Net Sales or Purchases					
Year	Outstanding (year end)	Change	Foreign(1) Countries	Gold Pool	IMF	Domestic Producers and Consumers
1953	631.2					
1954	622.7	- 8.5	- 9.3	—	—	+ 0.8
1955	621.5	-1.1	-1.9			+0.8
1956	630.2	+8.7	+2.3		+5.7	+0.7
1957	653.1	+22.8	+4.9		+17.1	+0.8
1958	588.1	-65.0	-65.5			+0.5
1959	557.3	-30.7	-28.5		-1.3	-0.9
1960	508.7	-48.7	-56.3		+8.6	-1.0
1961	484.2	-24.5	-27.5	-0.3	+4.3	-1.0
1962	458.8	-25.4	-21.3	-2.5		-1.6
1963	445.6	-13.2	-19.2	+8.0		-2.0
1964	442.0	-3.6	-12.3	+11.2		-2.5
1965	394.5	-47.6	-37.8		-6.4	-3.4
1966	378.1	-16.3	-13.9	-3.4	+5.1	-4.0
1967	344.7	-33.4	+2.9	-32.3	+0.6	-4.6
1968	311.2	-33.5	-6.0	-25.9^2	+0.1	-1.5^2
1969	338.8	+27.6	+27.3		+0.3	
1970	316.3	-22.5	-18.0		-4.5	
1971	291.6	-24.7	-24.1		-0.6	
1972	276.0	-15.6	-0.1		-15.5	

1973	276.0					
1974	276.0					
1975	274.7	-1.3				-1.3[3]
		-356.5	-304.4	-45.2	+13.3	-20.2

Note: Details may not add to totals due to rounding.
 Official foreign monetary institutions..
[2] Sales to gold pool and to U.S. consumers ended March 18, 1968.
[3] Gold sold at public auction on Jan 6 and June 30, 1975.

Comment: The table attached is Table E found above. While Treasury's answer to this is unsatisfactory, ironically, there was a perfectly good answer it could have given. It could have explained that the gold that went to the United Kingdom by plane in late 1967 did so in response to a run on the overvalued British pound. The gold was shipped in an emergency to try to shore up the pound. But years of British economic mismanagement could not be erased. The pound was devalued on November 21 from the $2.80 level it had held since 1949 to $2.40. Again, this was an historic event. Within weeks, many currencies were under market attack and fluctuated widely, and gold's price began to move out of the government's control. All these years later, that era of unstable paper currency value is still with us.

The Treasury's incomplete response gives added fuel to the question's very premise: That the Treasury hasn't given straight answers.

Allegation # 3		Treasury's Response
"Officials of the U.S. Bureau of the Mint admitted that shipments to England did take place in 1967 but would not say how much."		There was a brief period in late 1967 when the demand for gold in the London market was so great that in order to supply a quantity sufficient to hold the price at the approximate level of the official price (in accord with an international understanding in which the U.S. was participating at the time) it became necessary to ship 14,289,517 ounces in gold directly from Fort Knox to London. This required truck convoys and military aircraft to fly the gold to the U.K. In order to avoid giving speculators information on the amount being sold by the authorities which they could use for private gain, the physical shipments from Fort Knox were not made public at the time. All these shipments were authorized by the Secretary of the Treasury and were in accordance with announced U.S. gold policy. The Treasury received full payment for the gold valued at $35 an ounce, and the resultant reduction in the U.S. gold stock was reflected in the published statistics. Information on changes in the gold stock was published monthly with a time lag of approximately five weeks.

Comment: Satisfactory. But it is interesting to point out that the Treasury has often used its wish to avoid giving speculators information which could be used for private gain as its reason for not releasing figures. Yet it is a market truth, demonstrated time after time, that when the investment market senses that a value is artificial (in this case, the artificially high value of the pound in early November of 1967) no amount of government intervention can alter things. Betting against the government in the investment arena when the government is trying to repeal economic laws has made many investors fortunes. It is only sad that the wealth thereby transferred (in this case, gold) came, in the last analysis, from the American people, and went, via this London action, into the hands of big and sophisticated speculators. It is also ironic, because it was ostensibly to remove gold from the hands of speculators that the people's gold was confiscated in the first place back in 1933.

Allegation # 4		Treasury's Response
"In the period from 1966 to September of 1972 alone, the U.S. Government sent 143,342,857 troy ounces of fine gold to foreign governments. In return the U.S. received credit at a rate of $35 per ounce or a total of $5 billion. Today, [1976] that gold is worth $23 billion. The loss during this six year period: $18 billion."		Between January 1, 1966 and September 1972 the U.S. Treasury sold 31.9 million ounces of gold to official foreign monetary authorities (net), 14.5 million ounces to the International Monetary Fund and 61.6 million ounces to the London Gold Pool...all sales to governments were made at $35 per fine ounce consistent with the provisions of the Gold Reserve Act of 1934, which allowed the par value of the dollar to be set at $35 per fine ounce.

Comment: The Treasury's response *admits* that the gold was sold for $5 billion and simply ignores the fact that it should have been sold at a much higher price. This response defends a policy based on a 1934 statute which was unreasonable and which prudent officials should have sought to change. All this policy served to do was to deliver millions of ounces of gold into the hands of big and savvy investors who realized that the $35 per ounce price of gold was artificially low and could not be maintained forever.

Allegation # 5		Treasury's Response
"During the past 20 years the U.S. Government has shipped tons of gold to England and Europe. Yet today, the combined gold reserves of all European nations do not remotely equal the amount of gold the U.S. Treasury Department claims it shipped there. The obvious conclusion is that some of America's missing gold may have been routed into private hands instead of the depositories of foreign governments."		There is no reason whatsoever why changes in the gold reserves of European nations should equal the value of gold shipments by the U.S. to England and Europe. Gold sold for London Gold Pool operations was intended for resale to private citizens. Much of the gold initially sold by the U.S. to monetary authorities of foreign countries was resold by them to the IMF. Consequently, the reserves of the European nations would not reflect the total amount of gold sold to them. (It should also be borne in mind that most of the gold sold by the U.S. to foreign monetary authorities has been held by them on earmark by the Federal Reserve Bank of New York and has not been physically "shipped" out of the United States.)

Comment: Again, the Treasury admits the basic allegation. Officially Washington never denied that U.S. gold "may have" gone into private hands. In fact, that was the intention all along. Washington set out in 1961 to keep gold's artificially low price sacred. It did this for years by providing one ounce of gold for every $35 turned in to the Treasury gold window by a foreign government, broker, or individual acting through a foreign broker. Not until 1968 did the rules change to permit only foreign governments to claim U.S. government gold. And not until 1971 did the government stop the gold flow.

Allegation # 6		Treasury's Response
"The U.S. Treasury used the London Gold Pool from 1961 to 1968 as a cover to get rid of most of the U.S. gold reserves... and now they are counting gold assets that were shipped out long ago."		The statement which alleges that the shipments of gold to London for the Gold Pool arrangement were used as a cover for secret losses of U.S. gold simply isn't true. The London Gold Pool functioned between 1961 and 1968. It was an arrangement among U.S., Belgium, France, Germany, Italy, Netherlands, Switzerland and the U.K. to stabilize the price of gold around the official price by buying and selling gold in the London private market and was well publicized At times the pool operations resulted in net purchases of gold by the U.S. but at times it involved net sales. When the arrangement was

		terminated by the Washington agreement of March 1968 the U.S. had made net sales to the pool during its period of operation totaling 45.2 million ounces. (Between 1961 and 1965 the U.S. made net purchases of gold from the pool totaling 16.4 million ounces. Between January 1, 1966 and March 1968 there were net sales of 61.6 million ounces.)

Comment: Not a satisfactory answer. A definition of the London Gold Pool doesn't answer the allegation's final sentence. One is left with the impression that the Treasury doesn't know for sure exactly how much gold is held as assets, but in any event, the question is not whether there were "secret" losses, but whether the admitted losses were justified by any rational policy.

Allegation # 7		Treasury's Response
"A year ago when... questioned whether gold was missing from Fort Knox, the General Accounting Office conducted a limited audit at the facility, However, the GAO report on the results of that audit proved nothing."		The Bureau of the Mint has primary responsibility for the protective custody of gold stored at Fort Knox and other Mint field facilities. Title 31, U.S.C. 354 provides that at the Mints and Assay Offices there shall be made annually a general settlement of accounts under the immediate supervision of a committee appointed by the

Director of the Mint. As a result of this provision of law, the Director of the Mint appoints annual settlement committees which are composed of persons who are experienced in the various phases of handling bullion, and are chosen from the various field offices and the Director's Office in Washington, D.C. Those serving on the settlement at one institution are selected from the personnel of other Mint institutions.

The members of the committee verify the amount of all gold not under seal and inspect all joint seals attached to sealed compartments to insure that the seals have not been disturbed and the contents have remained intact. After verifying the exposed gold, the committee places all gold not required for current operations in a compartment, which is then sealed. This procedure is called "official Joint Sealing" inasmuch as the top official of each Mint Office being checked has representatives who witness the verification of the assets being checked and who sign the seal with the Director's representatives. Compartments under "joint seal" may be opened only upon written authorization from the Director of the Mint. Auditors representing the Comptroller General observe the annual settlements as his office sees fit. In short, the administrative procedures for securing and verifying gold under Treasury custody are very secure and in full conformity with the law. Given these procedures there is simply no reasonable possibility that there is any truth whatsoever to the allegations that gold was unlawfully removed from the U.S. gold stock. To remove any possible lingering doubt on the part of anyone, Secretary Simon extended an open invitation to all members of Congress to conduct a personal inspection of Fort Knox or any other Federal gold depository. Seven members of Congress accepted this invitation and an inspection with complete press coverage was held on September 23, 1974. In addition, General Accounting Office and Treasury auditors completed an audit of the government gold stock requested by Congress. In its report, issued in February 1975, the GAO concluded that the 147,353,027 ounces of gold held at Fort Knox as reported on June 30, 1974 by the Bureau of the Mint was correct. The audit involved opening three compartments and counting and inspecting 91,604 gold bars from which random samples were taken to be assayed for their gold content. These bars represented approximately 21% of the gold stored at the depository or 11% of the total gold stock. The audit confirmed the records of the Bureau of the Mint for those compartments. No counterfeit gold was found.

In June 1975 the Secretary of the Treasury directed that a continuing audit of all United States-owned gold for which the Treasury Department is accountable be undertaken. This continuing audit is being conducted by ad hoc committees under the general direction of a Continuing Committee for the audit of United States-owned gold. The Continuing Committee includes representatives of the Treasury's Bureau of Government Financial Operations, Bureau of the Mint and the New York

		Federal Reserve Bank. Continuing audits were undertaken in fiscal year 1976 with the objective of inventorying at least 10% annually. In the event that differences are found, the time frame and approach will be re-evaluated. At the end of April 1976 the audit had accounted for over 10% of the 274.7 million ounces of United States-owned gold. The General Accounting Office observed the audits and expressed no objection to the procedures followed.

Comment: I've discussed the audit in Chapter Nine and still believe it was unsatisfactory, as is this response. Random samples are just not good enough. Regarding the last sentence of the second paragraph: To many people, a continuing committee of overseers composed of people of the sort described would be tantamount to allowing students to grade their own papers. Besides, focusing on the minutiae of the audit does not answer the question of why so much gold was allowed to leave the U.S. in pursuance of an unworkable policy for so long.

Allegation # 8		Treasury´s Response
"The GAO auditors confirmed that gold was stored in the three vaults they inspected but did not analyze core borings of the bars to determine purity-which is general procedure in most audits."		Chip samples from bars in the three compartments were assayed. The gold industry considers this method just as acceptable as drill samples as a method of assaying a gold bar without remelting.

Comment: Assaying only chip samples isn't good enough. We want to believe what Treasury says is true, but there have been too many governmental evasions in this area, as well as cover-ups in other areas of government. As the saying goes, "trust, but verify." We must be sure. Given the gravity of the allegations, why won't the Treasury use a method that will finally dispel the doubts?

Allegation # 9		Treasury´s Response
"What is left in Fort Knox represents only the dregs of what once was the greatest gold hoard ever gathered by men. Treasury Secretary William Simon has admitted that gold at Fort Knox is of "inferior quality." Specifically, it is "melted coin" gold, so full of impurities it is not acceptable for trade on the world market."		The bulk of the gold held in Fort Knox and the other mint depositories is in the form of coin gold bars. These bars contain approximately 90% pure gold and 10% copper. They were obtained by melting gold coins, most of which were surrendered to the Treasury in accordance with the Gold Reserve Act of 1934. They have been in this form since they were deposited in Fort Knox. Each bar is stamped to show its gold content and only the gold content

		is counted in U.S. gold statistics. No problems are encountered in selling these bars for their assayed pure gold content minus the cost of refining them to bring them to the fineness of bars normally traded on the organized exchanges and used in industrial production. While the Treasury could, no doubt, have the bars refined before sale when the cost of the refining is taken into account, the net return to the Treasury would be approximately the same as the return from the sale of the coin gold bars.

Comment: The Treasury admits the main point: Only the dregs of the once huge gold reserves remain. However, the allegation is wrong in its last assertion. A gold bar full of the impurities admitted by the Treasury would be acceptable on world markets, but only at a discount. In any case, the Treasury admits here that most of the bars fall into this category. They are at best only 90% gold. Just how much less gold is contained in them can only be ascertained by a complete inventory and assay.

Allegation # 10		Treasury's Response
"...some of the bars at Fort Knox may contain alloys other than gold...this concern [is based] on the fact that a bar of gold placed on scales during a public inspection of Fort Knox [in] September weighed only 22 pounds. A bar of fine gold is supposed to weigh 27 pounds. Obviously either the scales were wrong or there was something other than gold in that particular bar..."		The 22-pound bar of gold that was consideredunderweight mentioned in the [allegation] was a coin gold bar weighed on a household scale during the Congressional inspection of the Fort Knox depository on September 23, 1974. Coin gold bars are lighter in weight than the standard fine gold bar because of their copper content. They are also subject to a 10% variation in weight, as are all bars, due to the casting process. These factors can bring the weight of the coin gold bars to near the 22-pound level.

Comment: The idea that the best scale Fort Knox could come up with was a common kitchen scale staggers the mind. However, the Treasury is correct that the weight of a bar on a kitchen scale would not be recorded accurately. But the fact remains that the bars are substandard.

Allegation # 11		Treasury's Response
"No mention was made of the fact that the central core vault at Fort Knox (which was specifically constructed to house the nation's gold supply) was empty-a fact later confirmed by an official of the Treasury."		Allegations relating to the so-called "central core vault" are grossly inaccurate. No major alterations have been made to the main vault since construction of the depository was completed in 1936. We find no record

A similar allegation...
stated that "in 1942-
43, Major Stanley
Tatom designed
and oversaw the
construction of a
central core vault,
below the main vault.
To get to this ultra
safe vault an elevator
had to be installed
and it used up the
space occupied by
twelve of the former
vault compartments.
This explains why the
numbering in the
vault compartments
upstairs had a 12-digit
gap.

that Treasury officials
have ever referred to
any part of the Fort
Knox depository as a
"central core vault".
The elevator was
installed at the time
the depository was
constructed in 1936.
There is no record
of a Major Stanley
Tatom designing
or overseeing any
construction at the
depository. The
visitor's log at the
depository does show
the name of a Major
Daniel F. Tatum as
calling on the Officer
in Charge on July
20, 1942. We also
have records which
show that a steel
door was erected
by the Champion
Wire and Iron Works,
Louisville, Kentucky,
at the entrance to
the corridor that leads
to compartments
numbered 1 through
14 in the basement
level of the depository.
This work was
completed on
January 1, 1942 and
the number 15 was
assigned to the door.
After this work was
completed gold was
stored in the corridor
temporarily during
which time the door
was locked and
sealed. The records
further show that the
depository had 28
compartments at the
time of construction.
The compartments
on the lower level
were numbered

		1 through 14 and the corridor door was number 15 when it was added in 1942. The compartments on the upper level were numbered 21 through 34. There is no record of the numbers 16 through 20 ever being used on vault compartments at the depository and therefore no "12-digit gap" due to the alleged central core vault.

Comment: Again, the response is not completely satisfactory. We are, in fact, willing to believe that there have been "no major alterations" made to the main vault since original construction. However, the policy of not allowing any outsiders in (even participants in the 1974 tour were limited to specially chosen areas) and the fact that the Treasury has been evasive in so many responses naturally engenders any number of rumors about possible funny business inside Fort Knox.

The last allegation addressed by the Treasury in May 1976 concerned the "60 pounds of plutonium" allegedly stored at the Fort Knox Depository. Plutonium is a radioactive substance, and reports were circulating at the time that leaks were contaminating the surrounding areas. The Treasury's response asserted that no plutonium was stored there and that a special U.S. Army survey conducted the previous November had found no radioactivity.

While this response is probably true, such rumors spring from the great secrecy characteristic of all matters pertaining to Fort Knox. If the vault and all gold records were opened completely to qualified outside observers, these allegations would be satisfactorily answered.

As it stands, not many of these 12 allegations met with satisfactory answers. This is especially remarkable when you realize that the Treasury itself chose exactly which of the questions it would answer. In all the research I have done, I have not seen a good answer to the question of why qualified outside observers can't be let in to look. Treasury says it would cost too much (this from the same people who spend a millions of dollars every second), or they invoke security reasons, as if the blue-chip observers could not be completely screened by the FBI.

Overall, a careful analysis of the Treasury's responses leads to the conclusion that as many questions are raised as answered. In any case, never since have officials attempted such a complete response, and certainly never again would Nixon-Ford officials attempt to explain what went on. A few months later they would be voted out of office.

Chapter Eleven

CARTER ADMINISTRATION RESPONSES

Acting in the belief that a new administration would want to see if all was well after eight years of Republican rule, Jimmy Carter's new Treasury Secretary was asked to look into any possible irregularities of previous administrations. This proved to be a naive request, because, although administrations had changed, the same Treasury bureaucrats remained. From these officials came replies couched in the same language as before.

For example, addressing on March 8, 1977 the question of why there should be no independent audit, Mr. Jerry H. Nisenson (Deputy Director for Gold Market Activities at the Treasury's Office of Foreign Exchange Operations) wrote: "A continuing audit of all United States-owned gold is currently in progress. These audits are being conducted on a cyclical basis because of the enormous quantity of gold to be physically handled and the related costs. The Government personnel conducting these audits are highly qualified and experienced in the various phases of handling bullion. To date, the audits have accounted for over 20 percent of the total U.S. gold stock. Representatives of the General Accounting Office, an organ of the Congress and completely independent of the executive branch, observed several of the audits and expressed no objection to the procedures followed. Thus, *there is simply no justifiable reason to secure the services of a private accounting firm."*

Evidently, no change in policy could be expected from the Carter White House. Indeed, Carter's policy turned out to be no better than that of his predecessors. In fact, a few months after Nisenson's letter was written, an event occurred which showed that President Carter's people would be *even less interested in candor* than were President Ford's.

The 1977 "Peek" at the Gold

After the Carter administration took office in 1977, one more public visit to Fort Knox vaults took place. On July 28, Treasury Secretary Michael Blumenthal spent less than two hours at the depository. He was shown only two vaults and, as we will see, had no intention of being objective about the question of whether all the gold was accounted for. His mind was already made up.

Secretary Blumenthal was in Louisville to deliver a speech about tax reform to the city's Chamber of Commerce. He delivered the speech immediately after "inspecting" Fort Knox, and here is how he began:

"If I appear a bit dazzled, I hope you'll forgive me. I've just been down the road to inspect the nation's gold stock at Fort Knox.

"First, I can report it's still there. If that comforts you, think what it does to me—the man who has legal responsibility for its security."

Blumenthal's speech starts out wittily enough, until you realize that these remarks had been written in Washington and even distributed to the press at least a day before they were read in Louisville. Blumenthal had entered Fort Knox knowing exactly what he would "report" to the public. (It is common practice for the texts of the speeches of politicians and officials to be distributed to the press beforehand, with the understanding that no contents be released to the public until after the speech is given. I have a copy of Blumenthal's text plainly prepared well in advance of his visit.)

In 1977, Blumenthal was indeed "the man who [had] legal responsibility for" the security of the nation's gold reserves. We now wish that he had taken these responsibilities a bit more seriously.

The next few paragraphs of Blumenthal's speech that day show what official Washington thought of gold and sound economic policies. The Secretary continued:

"Second, it's [the gold Blumenthal had just 'inspected'] beautiful and impressive. But I couldn't help but reflect that the great pile of gold there is a monument to a by-gone era in monetary policy and economic thinking.

"Today it plays no role at all in U.S. domestic monetary policy— and virtually every country in the world has agreed to reduce its role in the international monetary system.

"In the old days of commodity money, people believed that the strength of a currency depended on the country's stock of gold or other monetary commodity. But we understand today that the value of our currency, at home and internationally, depends not on our holdings of those metals, but on our *fundamental economic performance* ... a strong dollar is of major importance . . . and the only way to assure a strong dollar, both at home and in international money markets, is by *following sensible economic policies, by keeping inflation under control* and introducing an effective program for conserving energy and by improving the vitality and efficiency of our economy. *The Carter Administration is following this approach, and I am happy to report that recent indicators show continued and welcome progress.*"

We all know how Blumenthal's report of "continued economic progress" turned out in actual fact. The Carter Administration was swept out of office in 1980 after the prime interest rate reached 21% with inflation rates not much below that. Carter's "approach" landed the U.S. economy into what was then the worst recession since the Great Depression. And, even though Blumenthal attacked gold's importance, over three decades later gold's reputation is far higher than that of the Carter Administration's economic policies.

Questions About the Gold Remained

Blumenthal said he was "happy to report "that the gold was "still there." That report still remains to be verified.

But the Blumenthal visit accomplished what it was meant to do. A few paragraphs appeared in *TIME* magazine (August 8, 1977) along with a picture of "Blumenthal Fondling His Treasury." Once again, an opportunity to reassure Americans about their gold reserves was missed—or purposely avoided.

By the second year of the Carter Administration, all interest in polite responses to repeated queries seemed to vanish.

This was the case with Congress, as well. For instance, when Ohio industrialist Edward Durell tried to draft letters of inquiry to be sent under the signature of an old acquaintance (and campaign finance recipient) Ohio Representative Bill Stanton, he was surprised at the response. Stanton, obviously not wanting to rock the boat, declined to put his signature on a letter he did not write. "It would be morally wrong, my taking your letter and sending it as if it were my very own," he said. This is, of course, exactly what Congressmen do all the time when their staff members write letters for them.

Durell sent the letters himself, and got the following response from the General Accounting Office. The subject was the adequacy of the GAO's audit, and the response, excerpted below, basically boils down to a "take it or leave it" attitude:

"How audits are conducted, must, in the final analysis, rest to a large extent on the judgment of the auditors. We have given you our reasons why we conducted the audit in the manner that we did. We have nothing more to add. Judgments are always open to question. For our part, we believe we made an adequate audit employing proven techniques, including statistical sampling procedures. With that you obviously disagree. We respect your right to do so."

More brush-offs were received during the waning Carter years, from Federal Reserve Chairman-designate G. William Miller and Senate Banking Committee Chairman William Proxmire. They both promised to look into matters. Nothing more was heard.

A Hint at the Disarray Below the Surface

One episode in particular dramatizes why increasing numbers of citizens were unwilling simply to trust the government's pat assurances. The story broke on December 21, 1978, when several newspapers published this report: "The U.S. Treasury Department announced yesterday that more than 433 pounds of gold worth $1.1 million is unaccounted for at its New York Assay Office. . . ." (From *NEWSDAY*)

Two days earlier, on December 19, 1978, Deputy Treasury Secretary Robert Carswell wrote to Senate Banking Committee Chairman William Proxmire referring to the assay office irregularities and stating: "The full truth may never be known because of the inadequate records kept over the years."

Yet, the Treasury closed its investigation on August 7, 1979, as reported by the *Wall Street Journal*: "The great U.S. Treasury missing gold case is closed—but it isn't solved.

"The agency said it completed its investigation into its New York assay office, which the Treasury said 'lost' about 4,100 ounces of gold, valued at almost $1.2 million at current prices, between 1973 and 1977.

"But because of shoddy recordkeeping at the office, the Treasury said it couldn't determine whether the gold was stolen or was lost through normal processing. The agency said it caught one employee, who is in prison, removing 600 ounces of gold and has recovered 250 ounces. But there isn't any evidence other employees were involved in theft, the agency said.

"Last December, the Treasury said it had lost an estimated 5,200 ounces of gold. Since then, it has 'identified and corrected' some 'recordkeeping and procedural irregularities' and 'security problems' at the office, the Treasury said yesterday."

Reagan Stirs New Hope

President-elect Ronald Reagan's talk of a gold standard raised high hopes that the new President would move on the Fort Knox controversy.

Transition members of the new administration were contacted. James Baker was polite, but non-committal. In December 1980, Reagan's friend Paul Laxalt "commended [the questioner] on your persistence in attempting to get an inventory of the nation's alleged gold reserves. The information you have appears as though it could provide the public with some interesting side facts into the nation's gold reserves. I will definitely keep your thoughts in mind and will refer your mailgram to President-elect Reagan's transition office."

But when the Reagan people moved in, a disappointing (yet familiar) story began to emerge. One citizen, M. L. Hendricks of Lincoln, Nebraska, wrote to Treasury Secretary Donald Regan soon after he took office urging an inventory of the gold stock.

On March 13, 1981, almost four years to the day after he'd written last, our old friend Jerry H. Nisenson of the Office of Foreign Exchange Operations gave his standard reasons for why a real audit couldn't be done.

In August, more concerned citizens got form letter responses to their inquiries. They were signed by Donna Pope, the new Director of the Mint. She may have been new, but her answers were not. The last paragraph of her form letter reply stated: "There is ample evidence in recent audits to show that any allegations concerning the nonexistence of gold at depositories and institutions are irresponsible and unfounded. The Treasury Department has gone to extraordinary lengths to reassure the American people that no gold is missing and the gold stock is being managed responsibly."

Needless to say, nothing in the letter gives complete satisfaction.

Any Way to Treat a Reaganite?

The best attempt at a response during the Reagan era came as a result of a letter to the President from Mr. Robert Pratt, an air traffic controller from Topeka, Kansas. For decades, public sector labor unions had been striking and holding the American economy hostage. Months after Reagan was elected, PATCO, the air traffic controllers union, went on strike and members were shocked when Reagan responded by immediately firing anyone who had participated.

Just days after, on September 3, 1981, Pratt wrote a letter to congratulate President Reagan for "the firm action" he had taken. "Government employees should not have the right to strike," said Pratt. ". . . . I am not on strike because my facility is not, but even if it were, I still wouldn't be on strike." In Reagan's mind, Pratt was an unsung national hero. His letter undoubtedly gave Reagan much-needed support at the time, and thus it stood not only an excellent chance of meeting his eye, but also of promting a response.

What makes Pratt's letter interesting for our purposes is his last paragraph: "I request [that] you appoint a Blue Ribbon Presidential Commission of Inquiry to investigate the reasons why no complete, physical [and] assayed inventory of the nation's gold holdings at Fort Knox and other depositories has been taken for many years in spite of numerous requests."

Mint Director Pope responded to Pratt in an October 8 letter that "The President has asked me to respond to your letter , . . concerning an inventory of U.S.-owned gold." What followed was the usual response about the ongoing audit, then in its seventh year.

Very little of Pope's letter actually addressed Pratt's specific question of why no complete, assayed and physical inventory had taken place. After detailing how the audit operated, she said "The continuing audit is being conducted on a cyclical basis because of the enormous quantity of gold to be handled and the related costs. . . . It would not be feasible to complete a 100 percent audit within a six-month period, under the stringent control procedures required, without seriously impairing our audit of other vital Treasury operations."

This "response" is less than satisfying on several points. First, nowhere in Pratt's letter did he ask for an *audit*. He asked for an inventory. Government responses, however, always use the word audit, which implies a cursory "hearsay" proclamation that all the gold is there. *Inventory*, on the other hand, especially the "physical, assayed" inventory which Pratt requested, implies a thorough, bar-by-bar counting and surveying. In short, an audit is a review of the books; an inventory is an actual count.

The tendency of officials, in this and other responses, to put this different word into the mouths of questioners confuses the issue at the outset.

Moreover, nowhere in Pratt's letter did he request that such an inventory be made "within a six-month period." This was Pope's idea, and it further muddied the waters. Of course, compressing this "audit" into a six-month period would be costly, and take away personnel from other tasks. But who asked for a six-month audit? It didn't seem to matter to Pratt, nor would it have, how long the process would take. The important thing is that it be an honest process.

Mrs. Pope made her response even more murky when she alluded to the audits of "other vital Treasury operations" which a full gold audit would "impair." Exactly what "vital" operations would be impaired by an honest gold inventory was not detailed.

Turn to the Private Sector

In the next sentence of her letter to Mr. Pratt, Mrs. Pope continued the government's policy of ignoring the only sensible solution to the gold question: An honest and independent audit. A real audit can't be done, she said, because of the "question of the availability of personnel with the necessary experience and qualifications...." But in the private sector there is no lack of qualified and experienced accountants and assayers available to do the job. Ernst & Young and PriceWaterhouseCoopers are just two accounting firms that could be retained.

As to independent assayers of gold, Johnson Matthey and Englehard both have impeccable reputations. My own personal choice would be Johnson Matthey, which has been in the business since 1817. With 8,500 employees worldwide, it is truly the "gold standard" when it comes to assaying. However, it is a British company, and for political reasons, a U.S. company may have to be chosen.

There is a new company in Virginia called Bullion Analysis (HYPERLINK "http://www.bullionanalysis. com/"www.bullionanalysis.com) which claims to have developed a new technology that revolutionizes the assay method. This tecquniqe can detect any impurity and cavity, even those hidden deep inside the bar. Moreover, unlike in the "old days" (before 2010) when assayers had to drill into the bar for samples or send it off to either a lab or a smelter, Bullion Analysis' method is completely non-invasive. (Indeed, for anyone who owns a bullion bar of precious metal and wants to be sure that is does not contain lesser metals like tungsten or lead, this company may be used.) Each bar is intensively scanned and a tamper-resistant holographic assay certificate produced. These certificates can trade with the bullion and offer both buyer and seller— or in this case, the owners, the American people— security. Technicians from the company offer to "travel to your secure depository and warehouse locations and perform the analysis under guard and your firm's supervision", so they would certainly be able to go to Fort Knox and their costs seem quite reasonable. Further investigation would have to be done before such a firm could be hired, but an American company using the latest technology would appear to be a perfectly good alternative.

New Jersey-based Englehard has only been in business since 1958, but it has the distinction of creating the first catalytic converters to reduce automobile pollution. (These use small amounts of precious metals.) In 2006, Englehard was purchased by Germany's BASF, the world's largest chemical company and I'm just not sure that Englehard's assaying capabilities are as good as Johnson Matthey's.

These outside, private firms would have nothing to gain, and everything to lose, by engaging in a cover-up. And yet, Mrs. Pope's letter to Mr. Pratt continued, "We have full confidence in the accuracy of our records..." Unfortunately, the public does not.

You don't have to believe there is a cover-up to be unsettled by Pope's statement that she is satisfied with the accuracy of her own records. Who among us has never made an honest mistake, a mistake that was caught by an outside and objective observer? For such an important task as the inventorying of our nation's official gold supply, it seems *common sense* would indicate that the records be checked and that the operation be carried out by objective observers.

All of Mrs. Pope's irrelevancies and evasions, as well as her condescending attitude, were summed up in her letter's penultimate sentence: "Under the circumstances, we feel that any effort to compress the ongoing audit into a *substantially shorter timeframe* [who is in a rush?] would *clearly* [clear to whom?] jeopardize the audit of *other more vulnerable operations* [such as?] and would be a *waste* of taxpayer's money [many would disagree]... [Editorial comments added.]

So, to the Reagan Administration in 1981, Air Traffic Controller Robert Pratt may have been a hero for staying on his job and supporting his President's action at a critical time. But when he requested a lawful accounting of our nation's gold, he met with a response chock-full of slippery evasions and, further, one which contained more than a hint of ridicule and mockery.

"I hope you will find this information responsive to your inquiry."

So went Pope's sign-off to Pratt. Quite understandably, he did not. Some weeks after he received Pope's letter, he sent copies of it and all his "Presidential" correspondence to Edward Durell, Pratt's cover letter contained these resigned, and slightly ominous, words: "No doubt this reply is similar to others generated from your efforts but at least it can be added to your files. My very best wishes to you for your efforts in this work. I hope someday we will see a complete and honest audit. Although it may ruin the country."

Chapter Twelve

IRREGULARITIES HAUNT THE TREASURY DEPARTMENT

In the years since 1981, chinks in the Treasury's armor have given us frightening glimpses of what many have suspected throughout our story: That something is drastically wrong at the Department of Treasury.

Item: The American people's gold is the direct responsibility of the Treasury Department. Yet, not until February 6, 1984 did the Treasury have an internal watchdog against fraud or inefficiency. As the *New York Times* put it: "The House gave swift approval today to legislation that would create offices of inspector general in the Treasury and Justice Departments, the *only Cabinet agencies lacking such internal watchdogs against waste, fraud and inefficiency*."

Item: In a letter of April 24, 1987, from the Treasury's newly created Inspector General to Treasury Secretary James Baker, the Inspector, Michael R Hill, described how he canceled the ongoing audit because the full ten years had elapsed with 100% audited. He concluded that, "Moreover, annual independent audits of the gold were no longer necessary because virtually all of the gold in custody of the Mint had been audited and because there had been essentially no discrepancies found by audits made over the last 10 years." In other words, even though during most of this time the Treasury had no Inspector General to guard against fraud, the Inspector General says no independent audit is needed since the one initiated in 1975 was honest.

Item: The following singular report appeared in the Jack Anderson column of *The Washington Post* on February 11, 1976. It concerned Mrs. Mary Brooks, who we have met before in these pages:

"The strange case of the pilfered pennies helped to send earnest Mary Brooks, the harassed director of the U.S. Mint, to the hospital last November with nervous exhaustion. She is still quietly recuperating.

"Many pressures contributed to the strain that has kept her away from her office for more than three months. But the incident that upset her the most, according to friends, was the mysterious disappearance of a dozen aluminum pennies on Capitol Hill.

"The experimental coins were delivered to the Senate and House Banking committees for the members to inspect. That's the last the authorities saw of most of the pennies, which are worth thousands of dollars apiece to anyone brash enough to risk federal prosecution. Within a few years their individual value may be as high as $100,000.

"Poor Brooks was responsible for the rare coins. She had to get them back or report them stolen. But it would have been awkward for her to accuse members of Congress of theft. She would have been obliged to investigate the very committee members who oversee the U.S. Mint.

"We published the story of the missing coins on April 21. This put Brooks on the spot, but she was unable to solve the disappearance. Meanwhile, the light-fingered legislators still haven't returned the valuable coins.

"The embattled Mind director finally arranged for hospitalization last November and disappeared as quietly as the pennies. Her friends say she hopes to be back in her office in a few days on limited basis.

"All a spokesman at the Mint would say was that he expected the boss back in the office 'in a short time'."

This was the guardian of our gold stock? The same one who was saying "Trust us to safeguard it?"

Item: On December 11, 1978, the U.S. Treasury announced that over 433 pounds of gold were unaccounted for at the New York Assay Office, the only place where the government melted and refined gold. Said Joseph Laitin, assistant secretary of the Treasury, *"The full truth may never be known because the records are so poor."* In this case, two

New York Assay Office employees were ultimately charged with theft.

Item: Writing to Representative Ron Paul (R-TX) on November 7, 1983, W. Dennis Thomas, Assistant Secretary of Treasury for Legislative Affairs said of the unresolved assay irregularities: "We cannot state with absolute certainty that there were not additional thefts . . . as you know, the New York Assay Office was closed in December 1982." Everyone knows that for every government scandal that sees the light of day, there are many more that are hushed up. Certain conclusions spring to mind in light of the irregularities and even fraud that have recently emerged from the Mint and the Assay Office, the two bureaus most concerned with our gold.

Item: In April 1988, it was revealed by Rep. Frank Annunzio (D-Ill.) that the Mint has plans to withdraw the Army Forces now guarding Fort Knox and replace them with private security guards. Annunzio chaired the congressional committee that oversees the Mint, but he was never able to get an answer on this from the Treasury Secretary (Treasury is the Mint's "parent").

This means that the Treasury is planning to *reduce security at Fort Knox*. The San Francisco Mint was being guarded by private security guards in 1982, when it was discovered that some guards had been smuggling thousands of dollars worth of coins as they left the warehouse every day. Later, in 1985 thieves stole $14,000 worth of quarters from a warehouse under contract to the government but protected by private security guards.

So what does this change to lessened security mean? It could make it easier for someone to spirit away what gold remains at Fort Knox. On the other hand, isn't the very fact that security may be reduced a tacit admission from the Treasury that there isn't as much inside as they've led us to believe?

The Mystery Remains

These few items are simply the most recent testaments to an ongoing mystery that began almost eighty years ago, when FDR revoked the right of American citizens to own gold. As we have seen, this act launched the country on a course of inflation and undisciplined government spending, and allowed what was historically the world's largest accumulation of gold to slip through our fingers.

There must be investigations, full, independent investigations. Once and for all, the American people should know for certain:

Just why did the government dispose of over half our gold in trying to defend a policy that had to fail?

How many billions of dollars did we lose by insisting on selling gold at an unrealistically low price?

Just what is the *quality* of the gold remaining in Fort Knox? We know that an overwhelming percentage is not good delivery gold—how much is there and how bad is it?

Why have government officials refused to hold an independent audit and assay, with complete physical inventory, of all the remaining gold?

Why doesn't the Treasury release all the records of its gold dealings? If some of the records are shoddy or nonexistent, as Treasury officials have themselves claimed, should not this fact itself be brought out?

Clearly, gold has in recent years regained an importance in the minds of Americans it had not held for generations. For the good of the country we need to know the truth about our gold reserves.

About the Author

Chris Weber has been an investor since 1971. He is the author of several books including *Bailing Out a Bankrupt World, Getting Rich Outside the Dollar, How to Buy Precious Metals at Home and Abroad*, and others. During 1982, he assisted in researching, drafting, and editing the Minority Report of the U.S. Gold Commission, authored by Congressman Ron Paul and Lewis Lehrman. It was subsequently published as *The Case for Gold*. He currently writes the Weber Global Opportunities Report, an investment newsletter, and can be reached at goodasgold@weberglobal.net.

Throughout this book, I will be quoting from government officials. I know they can be boring. So what I'll do is to put in *italics* those most important parts. So from here on out, anything in italics is done so by me.

[1]Official foreign monetary institutions..[2]Sales through gold pool and to U.S. consumers ended March 18, 1968. [3]Gold sold at public auctions. [4]Gold sold in American Arts Gold Medallion Program.
Sources: Federal Reserve Bulletins, Annual Reports of the Director of the Mint, U.S. Department of the Treasury, December 1981. (NOTE TO CREATESPACE: Table A, Row 2, "Foreign Countries" should reflect Footnote 1, not 2.)

Made in the USA
Charleston, SC
30 June 2011